Sta

Dynamic Extent-Based Allocation Technique for Multimedia File Systems

Stanislav Sokolov

Dynamic Extent-Based Allocation Technique for Multimedia File Systems

A Memory Allocator's Approach

VDM Verlag Dr. Müller

Impressum/Imprint (nur für Deutschland/ only for Germany)

Bibliografische Information der Deutschen Nationalbibliothek: Die Deutsche Nationalbibliothek verzeichnet diese Publikation in der Deutschen Nationalbibliografie; detaillierte bibliografische Daten sind im Internet über http://dnb.d-nb.de abrufbar.

Alle in diesem Buch genannten Marken und Produktnamen unterliegen warenzeichen-, marken- oder patentrechtlichem Schutz bzw. sind Warenzeichen oder eingetragene Warenzeichen der jeweiligen Inhaber. Die Wiedergabe von Marken, Produktnamen, Gebrauchsnamen, Handelsnamen, Warenbezeichnungen u.s.w. in diesem Werk berechtigt auch ohne besondere Kennzeichnung nicht zu der Annahme, dass solche Namen im Sinne der Warenzeichen- und Markenschutzgesetzgebung als frei zu betrachten wären und daher von jedermann benutzt werden dürften.

Coverbild: www.purestockx.com

Verlag: VDM Verlag Dr. Müller Aktiengesellschaft & Co. KG
Dudweiler Landstr. 99, 66123 Saarbrücken, Deutschland
Telefon +49 681 9100-698, Telefax +49 681 9100-988, Email: info@vdm-verlag.de

Herstellung in Deutschland:
Schaltungsdienst Lange o.H.G., Berlin
Books on Demand GmbH, Norderstedt
Reha GmbH, Saarbrücken
Amazon Distribution GmbH, Leipzig
ISBN: 978-3-639-15482-5

Imprint (only for USA, GB)

Bibliographic information published by the Deutsche Nationalbibliothek: The Deutsche Nationalbibliothek lists this publication in the Deutsche Nationalbibliografie; detailed bibliographic data are available in the Internet at http://dnb.d-nb.de.

Any brand names and product names mentioned in this book are subject to trademark, brand or patent protection and are trademarks or registered trademarks of their respective holders. The use of brand names, product names, common names, trade names, product descriptions etc. even without a particular marking in this works is in no way to be construed to mean that such names may be regarded as unrestricted in respect of trademark and brand protection legislation and could thus be used by anyone.

Cover image: www.purestockx.com

Publisher:
VDM Verlag Dr. Müller Aktiengesellschaft & Co. KG
Dudweiler Landstr. 99, 66123 Saarbrücken, Germany
Phone +49 681 9100-698, Fax +49 681 9100-988, Email: info@vdm-verlag.de

Printed in the U.S.A.
Printed in the U.K. by (see last page)
ISBN: 978-3-639-15482-5

Abstract

This thesis investigates the efficiency of extent-based allocator design to satisfy file allocation requests in a CDN proxy cache. The allocator is based on the method inspired by the memory allocators, where free space is managed in chunks of varying size, or extents. The design is tested in a simulation, where a trace of allocation and deallocation events from a content server was submitted to the allocator. Content serves of this type experience high demands on throughput, so their file system must store files in the most efficient way possible. The bottleneck for content retrieval often lies on data transfer rates of the hard disks used in the server. To facilitate fastest possible transfer of a file, it must be read sequentially, in one operation. At the same time, given the large quantity of file, which are present on such servers, space wastage due to incomplete utilisation of large allocation units is not desirable. Our allocator design tries to achieve both, to a certain extent, mutually exclusive goals. The design was implemented and the results we obtained in the course of simulation, show that we managed to achieve these goals, creating an allocator that displays properties, favourable for contiguous file placement, while keeping space wastage at its minimum. Additionally, the allocator is memory-efficient and has small bookkeeping and computational overhead. The use of our allocator in a CDN proxy file system will allow to keep the data transfer throughput at maximum speed, while utilising the storage space in an efficient manner. The reader of this thesis will learn about the allocator semantics and have a detailed introduction into a specific allocation algorithm, QuickFit. This study outlines several venues of improvement and opens for a further empirical study of complete system, based on the allocator presented in this thesis.

Contents

List of Figures

List of Tables

Chapter 1

Introduction

1.1 Motivation

The motivation for this study lies in the nature of the majority of the modern file systems, which use a fixed block size defined at the time of file system creation. These blocks are then used independently of the actual request sizes. This leads to either (1) wastage of storage space or (2) slower system performance. In the first case extra storage is wasted when the request size is not an exact multiple of block size. This situation is known as internal fragmentation. If the block size is set to a very small value to minimise internal fragmentation, then the second case occurs, as a file needs to be split over a larger number of blocks, leading to additional bookkeeping overhead, associated with location and reading of individual blocks before the complete file is read or written.

CDN proxy caches present an especial challenge. The load on the file system as the expected throughput is very high, requiring an efficient, preferably contiguous, placement of files. At the same time such caches operate with a very large number of files, making it undesirable to waste space by using larger blocks.

1.2 Problem Description

The original goal of this thesis was to make a design suggestion to a file system, where block sizes could be varied on the fly and

1

to investigate the performance implications compared to the traditional fixed block size approach. During the research phase we came across a work by A. Iyengar et al. [IJC02], where a design, very similar to our own intended concept, was already outlined.

The allocation algorithm used in Iyengar's system comes from the memory storage Ph.D research done by C. B. Weinstock [Wei76]. In the conclusion of his thesis, Weinstock states that it would be interesting to analyse the application of dynamic storage allocation (DSA) techniques in a file system context. Further the author says that "it is clear that many of the techniques explored in this thesis are applicable to file systems, but the use of I/O devices will no doubt affect the relative performance of the methods". We have therefore shifted the attention of this thesis to investigate the applicability of DSA techniques to a disk allocator, while concentrating on the methods proposed by Weinstock and Iyengar. The application field of our thesis was at the same time narrowed down to the context of a CDN proxy cache file system.

Over time there has been done a lot of research in the area of file systems, ranging from simple data storage to the more complex journalling and database file systems. Much of this research resulted in actual implementations, which are in widespread use today. At the same time, and in parallel, there were conducted many research projects on memory allocation, for example in heap memory management, where space efficiency was prioritised. Though having many common denominators, these fields of research have seldom crossed.

In this thesis examine one system which uses aspects of both domains. Based on the concepts presented in that system, we propose several improvements, which are then implemented and evaluated by the means of simulation with favourable results.

1.3 The Structure of the Thesis

In this work we will be looking into usability, application areas and strategy variations of a special type of an allocator, which uses extents for space allocation.

In Chapter 2 we will look at the task of a CDN proxy, defining at the same time the requirements placed on its file system. We will also briefly describe two file systems, which can be used in a CDN proxy.

Several storage allocation concepts, which an allocator works with, are presented in Chapter 3. Then, in Chapter 4 we describe Quick-Fit allocation technique. First a general description is given, followed by a presentation of Iyengar's allocator. The chapter is finished with the detailed presentation of the variation of the QuickFit used in our allocator.

Chapter 5 presents the layout of a file system, concentrating on the design of the allocator. This chapter also outlines the context for the simulation.

The implementation details of the allocator and its simulation driver are presented in Chapter 6. For each allocator component we first describe the data structures, following up with a description of how our design translates into code.

Chapter 7 first gives an overview of evaluation tests, that our allocator is subjected to. The each test is described in great detail and the results are presented and analysed.

Finally, Chapter 8 summarises the work and the results and presents the possibilities for future development.

The appendixes include a glossary over the terminology used in the thesis (Appendix A), a presentation and analysis of the allocation trace used in the simulation (Appendix B), the complete source code of the allocator and the simulator (Appendix C) and several sample outputs of the simulation runs (Appendix D).

Chapter 2

File System Requirements for a CDN Proxy Cache

In this chapter we will set the framework for the thesis. We first present the concepts describing a file system. We then present the demands placed on a file system serving in a CDN proxy cache. The chapter is concluded with a short presentation of two files systems, which can satisfy such demands.

2.1 Basic Concepts

2.1.1 File

The definition of the term *file* varies depending on the perspective from which we look at it. An application knows how to interpret data stored within such object and can make decisions as to how the object should be accessed. A file system, on the other hand, would see the same file as an unstructured object, a sequence of bytes, holding no particular meaning. This is a definition covering most traditional file systems and is not entirely true in the case when we talk about database file systems or multimedia systems, which have some knowledge about the properties of the stored objects. This distinction is important as a file system can adopt a more intelligent placing policy, should it have the knowledge of a file's characteristics. These include the life expectancy of a file, its intended usage frequency and expected growth.

5

2.1.2 File System

The primary goals of a file system are to store a file in such a way that:

1. it utilises the available storage space efficiently;

2. it is stored and retrieved with highest possible throughput;

3. it can be located by some meaningful reference;

The way in which the different file systems achieve this varies, and many systems add other functions depending on the area of application.

It is worth noticing that the first and the second goals are conflicting. Finding the best placement for a file incurs additional computational overhead, whereas fast placement strategies often lead to considerable storage wastage, as we will see in Chapter 3.

Another task of a file system is to access the hardware, where the particular files are stored. In the prehistoric days of 1970's and early 1980's the main type of storage media was a variety of floppy disks. File systems were expected to interface the hardware on a low level, computing such parameters as sectors tracks and interleaving [Roa76]. Later hardware implemented much of the low-level control in its firmware, masking the actual physical placement of data from the file systems. Furthermore, in most modern operating systems, the hard disk device drivers are no longer part of the file system. A file system is thus presented with a logical addressing interface to a hard disk, such as Linear Block Addressing (LBA). Many hard disks still provide a Cylinder-Head-Sector (CHS) addressing mode, but the values used, no longer correspond to the physical geometry of the media and therefore provide no real value for the file systems, when it comes to determining the best placement with regard to such variables as rotational delay. It means that newer file systems mostly have to map the blocks associated with a file to the LBA value, which is then passed to the device driver or directly to the hardware. The use of LBA will be discussed later in Section 3.1.

A good file system must also show a substantial degree of fault tolerance. The information that has been committed to the hard disk, must be located even after a system failure, when some of the bookkeeping data might be corrupted.

2.1.3 Dynamic Files

Not all files' sizes are known at the time of creation. We think it would be correct to note that the majority of files will constantly grow in size or will undergo random writes. The following two sections investigate this problem in more detail.

Growing Files

Most files grow as they are written resulting in the need to allocate additional space. The most obvious solution to the problem is to postpone the write operation and thus the determination of the space requirements until later. It is done in *delayed allocation* in XFS [SDH+96] or *Optimised Batch Allocation* in the techniques described by Iyengar et al. in [IJC03, page 16].

However, the technique does not represent the ultimate solution, as writes cannot be postponed indefinitely. Relying on delayed allocation for too long will lead to extensive data loss in case of system failure. It also increases memory needed for buffers. Therefore, buffered data must be written back to disk at short intervals. At a moment of such combined write operation up to several files might still be growing in size. It is beyond the scope of this thesis give a solution to the presented problem, though two possible solution might be:

Reallocation of the file to another extent or

Extension of the size of the currently allocated extent, possibly after some prior defragmentation.

Sparse Files

Many of the aspects of growing files apply also for sparse files. This type of files do not get allocated disk space for areas that have not been written thus resulting in internal "holes". Sparse files usually result when the file pointer is pointed after the current end of file, and some data is written at that position. First of all, it must be carefully evaluated if the system should support sparse files in the first place. If used, sparse files can lead to increase in file fragmentation when the holes are written to and additional space needs to be allocated out of order with the previously allocated extents.

If the sparse file support is implemented, it is probably best to let the files become fragmented and fill the holes by the means of allocating new extents and linking them in the correct order. If a file becomes too fragmented, it can be individually defragmented by a background housekeeping process.

2.1.4 Buffer Cache

The buffer cache implementation on a particular operating system can lead to a complication if a file system is to incorporate an extent-based allocator. For example, Linux buffer cache [MEC$^+$] expects a file system to set a system wide block size upon mount. This presents a problem as the variation in extent sizes might potentially be unlimited.

Linux buffer cache has a feature that can potentially be exploited to implement a work-around – *buffer block grouping* that allows one to group cache blocks so that they be written in one physical operation. Thus, if buffer cache block size is set to the smallest possible extent size – the grain size (see Section 3.1) and then the grains are grouped, we can achieve a logical extent representation in the buffer cache.

2.1.5 CDN Proxy Cache

The task of a *Content Delivery Network (CDN)* proxy is to act as a middleman between the content server and a population of clients. Proxy caches are responsible for storing copies of the content from the central server, thus creating a distributed access point to the content being served.

All proxy caches have several common properties [Dav99]:

1. Reduction in the content server's link bandwidth consumption. By moving the content closer to the consumer, there are fewer request/response and data packets travelling from the server.

2. Elimination of access bottleneck and reduction in server load. Only proxy caches make direct requests to the server if the requested content is missing or becomes outdated. As once cache serve multiple users, the access point to the content server and the request load becomes distributed among the proxies.

3. Reduction in response latency, since the proxies are located closer to the clients.

4. Increase in fault tolerance. Even when the central server is temporarily down, its contents is cached and still available to the clients.

Proxy caches incorporate several different methods to keep their content up to date and report content usage back to the central server. If the content becomes obsoleted or missing, a proxy has two choices. It can forward a request to the central server. Alternatively, the request can be forwarded to a another proxy at the higher of equal level in the hierarchy [Dav99], as shown in Figure 2.1.

In this thesis we design an allocator, aimed to be used with a web proxy cache file system.

Web proxies have several demands and constraints placed upon them. As we have learnt from the analysis of the web access logs (see Appendix B), web caches operate with predominantly small- and medium-sized files. These files are requested with hight frequency and the clients expect very short response times. The files must therefore be organised in such manner that they are read from the heard disk at a maximum transfer rate. This can be achieved if each file occupies one contiguous segment of space. Additionally, files belonging to the similar request groups (i.e. to the same web page), should be placed physically close together. The allocator must therefore support some form of spatial awareness.

When the cached content becomes obsoleted, the proxies replace their copies with a new version of the same file. Similarly, if the

9

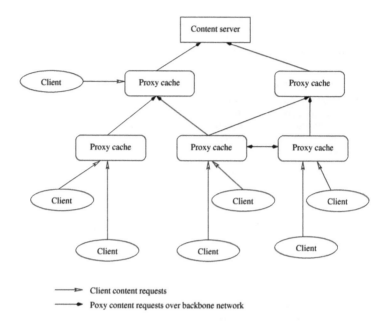

Figure 2.1: Proxy cache hierarchy

requested file is not present in the cache, it must fetch a new file and store it locally. If the free space becomes scarce or if some file are not requested for a long period of time, the proxy cache, must purge the files to free storage space. This indicates that the stored content is very dynamic, with frequent replacements and little correlation between the expected lifetimes of individual files.

2.2 Related Work

2.2.1 XFS File System

XFS [SDH+96, MEC+] is used in IRIX on Silicon Graphics computers. It was designed by Silicon Graphics as a further development

10

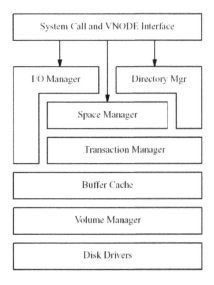

Figure 2.2: XFS architecture

of the Extent File System (EFS), when it became clear that EFS did not scale well to meet the new application demands, such as:

- fast crash recovery,

- ability to support large file systems,

- ability to support large, contiguous files and large directories,

- ability to support a large number of files.

XFS uses B$^+$ trees throughout the whole system. In XFS, extent is a contiguous number of free or used blocks. Each extent can contain a different number of blocks with a maximum of two million blocks, based on a 21 bit length field for the extent.

11

Allocation Groups

XFS introduces Allocation Groups (AG) to manage the file system more efficiently. Unlike cylinder groups in FFS, AGs are not designed to achieve greater locality. AGs can be considered as partitions inside a single file system - each AG has its own data structures for metadata and can be updated independently of other AGs, allowing for parallelism in file system management.

AGs have a maximum size of four gigabytes and in this way also reduce the address space for the metadata as pointers can be 32-bit values relative to the AG start. This saves space in metadata structures as XFS is a full 64-bit file system.

Free Space Management

To keep track of free space XFS uses a set of two B^+ trees for each AG. Both B^+ trees keep the descriptors of free extents as their entries. However, one of the trees is indexed by the starting block, and the other by the length of the free extent. The extents can contain different number of blocks. This allows efficiently finding the best match based on the type of allocation.

Support for Large Files, Directories and File Counts

XFS supports 64-bit address space for each file. This presents a problem if files are indexed by blocks. XFS solves this by using extent maps, where an extent is a number of contiguous blocks allocated to a file. However, in larger files with sparse allocation, the extent count can overflow the space left in the XFS inode. In this case, the remaining extent descriptors are managed through a B^+ tree rooted in the inode. This allows XFS to handle millions of extents each of which can be of a different size at the cost of an increase in computational complexity.

Furthermore, XFS supports a very large number of files. In [SDH+96], it is stated that the only real limit to the number of files is the available space in the file system. This is achieved by dynamically allocating inodes as they are required on the fly. As in previous cases, each AG manages its inodes separately from other AGs. A B^+ tree is used to keep track of chunks of inodes, each containing

64 entries. The inodes themselves can be either in use or free. Virtually, this strategy allows for allocation of an unlimited number of inodes at the cost of implementation complexity. Inode allocation, storage, and program interfacing are just some of the issues that must be addressed.

Directories in XFS use B^+ trees to store information about files. The keys for these trees are file names, which vary in size from 1 to 255 bytes. File names are hashed into 4-byte values which are used as the actual keys for the B^+ tree. The duplicate keys are resolved by placing such directory entries next to each other in the tree. Each directory entry contains the full name of a file along with the inode number. This solution increases complexity of the directory implementation, but improves the performance.

Variable Block Sizes

It must be noted that the block size in XFS is determined at the time of file system creation. XFS supports a wide range of block sizes from 512 bytes to 64 kilobytes.

Fault Tolerance

The system uses write-ahead logs to keep track of metadata transactions. This makes error recovery after a crash faster as it only need to recreate the system structures from the last checkpoint. A full-fledged system scanning can, nevertheless, be required in cases when logs or random blocks are corrupted due to hardware or software failures.

Performance

XFS employs delayed allocation techniques in which the blocks on the disk are reserved for the data in the buffer cache but are not allocated until the data are flushed. In this way, XFS is allowed to build larger extents before writing the data on disk, thus ensuring that files are stored as contiguously as possible. It is especially well-suited for random access pattern of write operations.

Delayed allocation in combination with the allocation of B^+ trees has the added benefit of keeping the file system fragmentation low by finding the best fitting free extents for the data as it is accumulated in the buffer cache.

2.2.2 PMFLF

Iyengar et al. presented in [IJC03] a new approach to organising files, which is very different from the traditional file system and database storage approaches. The storage management system is centred around an allocator, which is based on QuickFit allocation technique, borrowed from memory management systems. The file system itself keeps tracks of the allocated objects by the means of an on-disk hash table.

PMFLF is designed as a "parasitic" storage manager, intended to make use of an underlying file system to interact with the hardware. Its main strength lies in its allocator design, which we will present in great detail in Section 4.2.

2.3 Summary

XFS has a robust and efficient design. It, however, relies strongly on delayed allocation to make the optimal placement decisions, which leads to high memory consumption for buffers. In this thesis we will introduce allocation hint to provide an alternative way of providing the allocator with additional information to make its placement decisions. As XFS uses B^+ trees for all internal data management, it leads to a complex design and implementation. In this thesis, we will use a lighter, but equally efficient data structure – skip lists. Throughout this thesis we will be using several terms, introduced by XFS. Among these are the notions of extents and 64 bit addressing. We will, however allow extents to use 63 bits for their size description, whereas XFS limits extent sizes to 21 bits.

PMFLF, while having a relatively efficient design, still keeps several of the aspects of the memory allocation domain, which are either sub-efficient or directly counter-productive in the disk space allocation context. Some of these aspects are the lack of ability to fragment files over several extents and a separate treatment of the wilderness (see Section 3.3). We will be addressing these issues in the following chapters.

Chapter 3

Storage Allocation Concepts

In this chapter we explain the terminology used in describing the various parts of the allocation process.

3.1   Extent Size and Grain Size

The allocator manages free space in contiguous chunks, which we call *extents*. An extent is a sequence of one or more consecutive sectors on disk. The size of an extent is an integral multiple of *grain size* and is expressed in the number of grains it occupies. Likewise, an extent's starting address is expressed in the zero-based number of grains, counting from the start of the partition. This addressing mode coincides with Linear Block Addressing (LBA) mode used in hard disks. The grain size is determined at file system creation time and cannot be adjusted afterwards.

The smaller the grain size is, the less of internal fragmentation (see Section 3.6.1) we experience. The ideal theoretical minimum grain size corresponds to the extent header size plus *one* byte of payload. Though the internal fragmentation will be non-existent in such scenario, this solution is not practical, because all hard disks perform their operations in integral number of sectors. To reflect the operations of the underlying storage media, i.e. hard disks, the system shall use the same grain size as the sector size – 512 bytes.

Modern hard disks can be several hundred of gigabytes in size. Furthermore, it is possible to create logical volumes, which span several physical disks, for example RAID system, whose size can

AS	Size field 63 bits long

Figure 3.1: Tagged Size (TS) header format

exceed a terabyte marker. The current trend is a continuous increase in storage capacity. Our system must be able to adapt to this development. We therefore choose to use 64 bit addresses. Extent size will be limited to 63 bits as explained in the next section. Both values are expressed in grains and not in bytes. This design decision allows us to have extents of up to 2^{63} grains of 512 bytes, equalling 4.2 million petabytes.

3.2 Extent Header

The information about an extent size as well as any additional information about the state of an extent has to be stored at some location on disk. The additional information we have to store currently includes only *allocation status (AS)* of an extent. The allocation status of an extent is a bit field, which is set to 0 when an extent is free, otherwise it has the value of 1.

The on-disk extent headers can either be physically grouped together or stored within each extent. The first option leads to scalability problems as extent header area must be initialised to be able to accommodate a predefined number of headers. When the pre-allocated space for extent headers is used, additional space must be allocated, leading to increase in bookkeeping complexity. The headers of adjacent extents will also become physically separated on the disk as new extents are created by splitting the old ones.

Iyengar et al. [IJC03] store extent headers within the extents and propose a *Tagged Size (TS)* method for the header format. This method is depicted in Figure 3.1 and will also be used in our work. The most significant bit is used for the AS field, while the remaining 63 bits accommodate the extent size information.

18

3.3 Wilderness

The as of yet untouched space at the end of a partition is called *wilderness* [Ste83] (also called *tail* in some literature). This region can be treated in several ways, depending on the adopted allocation policy.

For example, we can always allocate from the wilderness when no exact fit is found, thus carving into the free space and splitting it into smaller chunks. This method is advantageous when the majority of allocation requests are from a small set of sizes. As extents are freed, the pool of free extents that are likely to satisfy the upcoming requests becomes sufficiently large.

Conversely we can attempt to allocate from the already existing free extents, performing *splitting* and *coalescing* as necessary and using wilderness allocation as a last resort. The latter is known as *wilderness preservation heuristic* [KV85, WJNB95]. We will, however, see in Section 4.2, Figure 4.5, that wilderness does not always need to be the largest free extent.

We now examine some mechanisms to represent the wilderness.

In the simplest form, a pointer to the beginning of the wilderness can be kept by the system both on disk and in memory and updated each time a wilderness allocation is performed. To reduce the number of disk accesses the update of on-disk pointer is deferred and occurs once after a certain number of updates. This approach is taken by the authors of [IJC03]. The issue of error handling caused by crashes will be discussed in Section 3.4.

Another way is to introduce *wilderness flag*, which marks the header of the wilderness "extent" and allows the allocation algorithm to treat it in a special way.

Finally, we can avoid treating wilderness in a special way, by acknowledging that it can be considered as a very large regular extent. If we choose the strategy to always split the smaller extents before the larger ones are taken (within a reasonable threshold, as will be discussed in Section 4.3.2), then the wilderness preservation heuristic will be obeyed automatically. That way we do not need to keep wilderness flag or to specify wilderness size anywhere other than in the standard extent header, corresponding to the last extent in a partition. This will make the system simpler in both design and implementation.

19

This last mechanism is our preferred way of treating wilderness in our allocation system. This method is the opposite of what is done in [IJC03], and is explained in detail in Sections 4.2 and 4.3.3.

3.4 Error Recovery Mechanism

While discussing deferred updating of wilderness pointer, Iyengar et. al mention [IJC03] an error detection mechanism – *code bytes*. It is described only briefly. From what can be understood from the paper, code bytes are a part of the header and their value is set when an extent is allocated. Their value in unallocated extents is left undefined by the paper, but it would be reasonable to assume that the code bytes are cleared along with the AS field when an extent is freed[1]. It is not said how many bytes are used and the only selection criteria for their value is that the probability of having the same sequence in the data field should be low.

In our opinion, computational and storage overhead, introduced by the code bytes outweighs their benefit in the marginal increase in safety they provide. Code bytes seem to be suited best for identifying the start of the wilderness. Even then, there is a possible scenario, leading to failure. After a failure. the proposed algorithm assumes the wilderness pointer to be invalid and searches the wilderness for the first allocated extent. A random bit sequence in the wilderness can coincide with the chosen code bytes, thus marking an "extent" as allocated when it is not. Though the authors are aware of this situation, they state that only a small amount of space would be lost due to the erroneous allocation and the price of the persistent storage is relatively low.

The authors however do not seem to be aware that quite significant amount of space can be wasted, should a misinterpretation occur. This is due to the fact that the size field of the misinterpreted "extent" would contain garbage, whose numeric value can be quite large. Another scenario, which leads to failure and which is not described by [IJC03] is the following: Consider an extent that has been allocated from the wilderness and then deallocated. Several

---

[1]It is indirectly stated by the following sentence in [IJC03]: *"When a block is allocated from the tail, both the AS field and code bytes are modified on disk to indicate that the block is allocated."*

20

more extents are then allocated from the wilderness. Before the wilderness pointer is updated on disk, the system crashes. During the rebuild phase, the old wilderness pointer points to the unallocated extents, which the system might interpret as the start of wilderness. All the allocated extents after the first one then risk being re-allocated, thus corrupting the data already stored in them. This problem can be circumvented by using different code bytes for "taken from wilderness, unallocated" and "taken from wilderness, allocated" extents. The downside is that the probability of occasional appearance of code values in the data of the wilderness increases respectively. This probability could be made less than the probability of failure at the expense of disk space.

If the authors only introduced code bytes to facilitate deferred wilderness pointer writing, we perceive it as a too costly a work-around in terms of space consumed in each header. There exist more elegant and fail-safe techniques to perform error recovery, such as journalling. We therefore choose not to implement code bytes, but rather treat the wilderness as an ordinary extent.

3.5 Boundary Tags

Memory allocators with general coalescing often implement a mechanism, known as *boundary tags* [Knu73], where a block header is duplicated in the footer, which is consulted whenever an adjacent block is to be coalesced. While this mechanism improves locality of reference in the memory scenario, when applied to a disk manager, it introduces additional costly disk accesses, which are needed to update the footer. As we plan to perform deferred on-demand coalescing only when no sufficiently large extents can be located and are going to use coalescing-by-sorting technique (described in Section 4.3.4), boundary tags become redundant.

3.6 Fragmentation Types

As we discussed above, one of the primary functions of an allocator is to ensure space usage with as small wastage as possible. Fragmentation can serve as a measure of success in this task. We

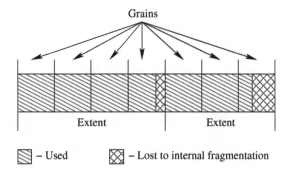

Figure 3.2: Internal fragmentation

discern between three types of fragmentation: *internal fragmentation*, *external fragmentation* and *file fragmentation*. The first two types refer to *free space* fragmentation and arise from inability to reuse existing free space [WJNB95, Bec82]. They are common for both hard space- and memory management systems. In contrast, the third type is specific for disks and does not fall under the definition given in [WJNB95] as it, strictly speaking, does not lead to waste of free space, but degrades performance of file accesses. Below we give the detailed descriptions of the different fragmentation types.

3.6.1 Internal Fragmentation

Internal fragmentation arises when an allocator serves a larger extent than was requested, because the extent cannot be split. This happens, for example, when the newly-created free extent would be too small or, more frequently after rounding up the requests to some integral value [Ran69]. Some space remains unused, but tied up *inside* the extent. This gives the origin to the name *internal* fragmentation. The situation is shown in Figure 3.2.

This type of fragmentation is common for both file- and memory management systems, but its causes are somewhat different. In most modern file systems, some level of internal fragmentation is always present as these systems use *blocks* of fixed size. A file system is therefore unable to adjust the amount of allocated space to the actual requests[2]. Some authors also count the space wasted on bookkeeping of extent data structures as part of internal fragmentation [WJNB95].

As an example, in a file system with a block size set to 2048 bytes, both requests for 500 bytes and 3000 bytes would produce internal fragmentation. In the first case $2048 - 500 = 1548$ bytes would be lost, while the loss in the second case is $2048 - (3000 - 2048) = 1096$ bytes in the second block. In general, internal fragmentation has also a far greater impact on the space utilisation in a file system as files have a longer life span than memory objects. The memory management systems are usually able to split blocks to meet the requests more accurately. Updates of the in-memory headers are also much cheaper than the on-disk updates.

Another cause for internal fragmentation is allocator's policy of being conservative with splitting in order to avoid external fragmentation.

3.6.2 External Fragmentation

External fragmentation occurs, when an allocator has free extents at its disposal, but none of the extents is large enough to satisfy a request and there are no adjacent free extents to merge to form a bigger contiguous free extent [Ran69, Bec82]. This situation is depicted in Figure 3.3. The typical cause for external fragmentation is when allocated extents of different sizes are deallocated after varying intervals of time.

This type of fragmentation is characteristic of the memory management systems. There, the allocator semantic promises that the returned space is contiguous. If merging of extents is not possible due to the allocator policy or the lack of adjacent free extents, then the storage is considered full even if the total number of free bytes

---

[2]Several file systems introduce mechanisms to reduce internal fragmentation. ReiserFS has a mechanism, caller *tail packing*, where data belonging to the last block or to files, which occupy less than a complete block are place together with meta-data. A similar mechanism for small file storage is adopted by NTFS. Both solution incur additional bookkeeping performance overhead and lead to increase in file fragmentation.

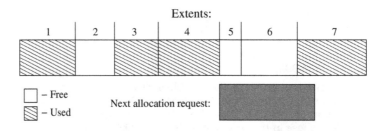

Figure 3.3: External fragmentation

could have served the request. While the internal fragmentation gradually saps the resources, the external type leads to an abrupt failure of a system, when some larger requests have to be rejected. It must be noted that the degree of external fragmentation in memory systems is dependent on the allocator policy and the chain of requests [WJNB95].

However, in the overwhelming majority of modern file systems it is possible to spread files over several extents. The external fragmentation is therefore replaced by another kind – file fragmentation, which is described in the next section.

3.6.3 File Fragmentation

As suggested in the previous section, file system allocators have an extra degree of freedom in object placement as they are allowed to scatter files over several extents. This is shown in Figure 3.4. Note that file fragmentation can arise in both extent-based and block-based systems.

Noticeably, there were file systems, which used contiguous file placement and did not allow file fragmentation. Among these are such legacy systems as RT11, NorthStarDOS and UCSD-Pascal [Roa76]. ISO9660 or CDFS, used with optical media, such as CD-ROMS, is an example of a newer file system.

File fragmentation, while effectively eliminating the external one, introduces a set of complications of its own. First, free space is still wasted – though negligibly – in the form of extra housekeeping

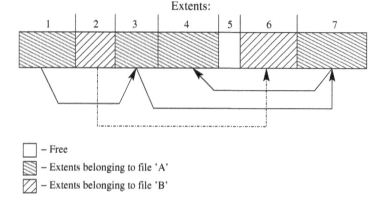

Figure 3.4: A simple case of file fragmentation

overhead at the file system layer. Second, sequential reading of a file is slower as all file fragments must be located and retrieved in a series of independent disk search operations, incurring extra seek time. Lastly, there is almost no correlation between spatial placement of extents and their deallocation times. Once a fragmented file is deleted, it is not likely that the adjacent extents, belonging to other files, will be freed as well, opening up the possibility for coalescing, before the next allocation request. This would prevent a subsequent contiguous allocation and further reinforce file fragmentation.

To illustrate this, consider Figure 3.4. If file 'A' is deleted, extents 1, 3, 4 and 7 will be freed. Though extents 3, 4 and 5 can be coalesced, file 'B' continues to be in the way of coalescing of extents 1 and 7. Moreover, a new allocation request for extents previously belonging to file 'A' can come long before file 'B' ever becomes deleted.

3.6.4 Conclusion

In this section we have looked at three types of fragmentation. These types are for the most part mutually exclusive in that an attempt to minimise one type, often results in increase of the other.

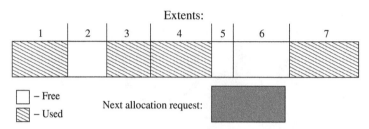

Figure 3.5: External fragmentation case, solvable by coalescing

A theoretical system that splits extents to the minimum size of 1 byte to avoid internal fragmentation will later be faced with a severe case of external one as smaller allocated objects become deleted at different moments in time.

Conversely, a system that avoids splitting extents at all costs, does preserve many large contiguous areas and is thus less likely to be faced with external fragmentation, while wasting a lot of space in internal one. It has in fact been shown in an empirical study of first-fit and best-fit allocators [Ran69] that it does not pay off to combat external fragmentation by rounding up requests to larger block sizes, as it leads to an even more severe case of internal fragmentation.

File fragmentation is in the first place used to combat external one, but has the disadvantages of (1) increasing the internal fragmentation by using an additional header for each extent, and (2) slowing down file access.

3.7 Defragmentation

As stated above, one of the important roles of an allocator is to combat fragmentation. It is done either implicitly, through the strategic choices made during the allocation phase, or explicitly, by performing housekeeping tasks.

3.7.1 Coalescing

During *coalescing*, adjacent free extents are merged to form a larger free extent. This operation can either be performed immediately after each deallocation to eliminate external fragmentation preemptively, or – as is done in most cases – deferring coalescing until the external fragmentation condition arises.

A typical case of external fragmentation, where coalescing would solve the problem is shown in Figure 3.5. In this scenario, enough space is available for the next request after extents 5 and 6 are merged during the coalescing procedure.

There are two types of cost associated with immediate coalescing. First, it adds computational complexity to the freeing stage as the neighbours of the just freed extent must be located and evaluated whether they are free as well.

Second, a less apparent cost comes from a highly probable redundancy of this task. Quite often the extents of a particular size or size range are needed. Especially in memory systems, there is a higher probability that smaller-sized blocks will be requested than large-sized ones, as the majority of programs display a tendency to require allocation of objects of small sizes [WJNB95][3].

Coalescing several small extents will therefore often have an effect that the newly-merged large extent has to be immediately split again to satisfy subsequent small-sized requests. In Section 7.2.6 we will investigate whether the same is true for our allocator.

3.7.2 Splitting

Another tool is *splitting* and it is used to combat internal fragmentation. Extents that are too large to serve a particular request are split into two smaller extents, one of which is returned to the pool. It is up to a specific allocator's policy to decide whether (1) an extent should be split to match the request exactly, or (2) the allocation request is rounded to the next higher multiple of grain size. Some

---

[3]This can be exemplified by the memory usage by our allocator. Some of the structures, for which it has to request memory are: extent headers, whose size is 16 bytes; the skip list header structures, whose size is 37 bytes; and skip list nodes, whose size varies between 8 and 136 bytes, depending on the type of the skip list (for implementation details, see Appendix C).

allocator policies can also decide if an extent should be split at all, based on the size of the remainder. This is known as *acceptable wastage* and is presented in detail in Section 4.3.2.

3.7.3 Relocation

As a rule, memory management systems cannot relocate objects to form larger contiguous free blocks. They simply do not have enough information to know where the object about to be relocated is referenced, and are therefore unable to update all references after a relocation. Object, or more precisely, extent relocation is, however, the approach taken by many file systems to combat file fragmentation. There are three ways perform defragmentation, depending on the desired outcome and the available time [Nor03].

We describe defragmentation for the sake of completeness, as we are not using defragmentation in our allocator design. The allocator does not have sufficient information about the usage of the allocated extents to perform defragmentation. Defragmentation is therefore the task of an external program, acquainted with both the file system and the allocator internals.

Defragmentation by relocation can be performed following these conditions:

1. a file is allocated for which no contiguous extent exists – free space must be compacted on the fly;

2. background defragmentation when disk activity and system load are below a certain threshold;

3. a user-requested defragmentation.

An algorithm described by K. Lund in his Master's Thesis [Lun97, chapter 9.2], is especially applicable in the first case as defragmentation must be performed as fast as possible and with the least impact on the system performance.

We discern between the following strategies for file defragmentation:

File defragmentation

File defragmentation does not aim at coalescing the free space. The files on a device are made contiguous, but are scattered throughout the whole partition, leaving the free space equally – or even more – fragmented. This method is relatively fast, but tends to worsen fragmentation in the long run as it leaves many small scattered free extents, which are later filled by fragmenting newly allocated files. It is best applicable to the systems with relatively constant content.

Free space defragmentation

The next method is *free space defragmentation*, which moves allocated extents to create one contiguous area of free space. Free space defragmentation is by several degrees faster than file defragmentation, but it only ensures that the files stored directly after the defragmentation process are contiguous. In contrast to the previous method, this one tends to worsen the fragmentation for the files already stored on a medium. It can nevertheless be useful if implemented appropriately, so as not to touch the files that are already contiguous. Free space defragmentation is the solution to the external fragmentation problem, presented in Figure 3.3.

File defragmentation with free space coalescing

File defragmentation with free space coalescing is the slowest, but the most thorough method, combining the strong sides of the two mentioned above. It completely reorganises the data on a storage device. As a result, all the files are made contiguous and grouped together in one section of a partition. Consequently, the remaining space is also compacted allowing subsequently allocated files to be contiguous too. There are several variants of this method, depending on where the files are placed. The files can either be placed at the start of the partition in a random order or spread over several groups, depending on the expected frequency of use. Due to the slowness of analysis and relocation processes this method is less suitable for use in a running system.

3.8 File Fragmentation and Multi-Extent Allocation

In an *ideal case* only one extent should be used for each file. This is however only possible as long as two conditions are met:

1. file size is known beforehand and

2. there is enough contiguous space or space that can potentially be coalesced to satisfy a request.

If either of the conditions is not met, the file might be spread over several extents. If the first condition does not hold, the system can potentially allocate too little space, so that if a file grows at a later point, there might not be enough space to accommodate it contiguously. This potentially leads to the situation where the second condition does not hold.

Though our target system has file sizes that are given at the time of creation, the life time expectancy of each individual file is still not known. After a sufficiently large number of file creations and deletions, the second condition might not hold. We are therefore forced to consider situations where the allocator has to allocate several extents for a single file to avoid external fragmentation, which introduces file fragmentation.

3.9 Summary

In this chapter we have presented the key concepts that are used in allocator design. These include both the parameters that an allocator works with and measures of allocators ability to efficiently manage the pool of storage space. We will be using these concepts in the next chapter, where we present an existing allocator design, and introduce our own improved allocator.

Chapter 4

Free Space Allocation Technique – Algorithm and Analysis

This chapter presents the free space allocation technique, which is used in this thesis – QuickFit.

4.1 QuickFit

The original version of Quick Fit algorithm can be found in Ph.d. thesis of C.B Weinstock [Wei76]. Weinstock and Wulf later presented the pseudo code of a modified version of QuickFit [WW88], where coalescing and splitting were removed from the algorithm. The same paper shows the application areas of QuickFit and argues for its efficiency in those cases. The algorithm was later adapted by Iyengar et al. [IJC03] for use in a disk storage allocator.

Quick Fit uses *segregated free lists* to store the references to free extents. Segregated lists is a general name for any free extent management structure, where free extents are assigned to different lists according to some policy. In our case, segregation criteria is the size of the extents.

There are two types of lists - *quick lists* (also called *exact lists*) and a *misc list*. Up to a certain threshold, there is a quick list for each extent size. Extents exceeding a threshold are grouped within a single

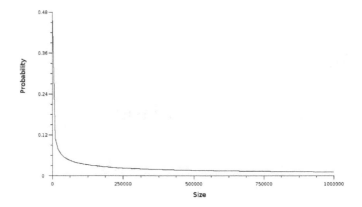

Figure 4.1: Optimal file size distribution for QuickFit

list - a misc list. This design is based on the assumption that file size distribution follows probability density of Pareto distribution, shown in Equation 4.1, which is skewed and heavily tailed (see Figure 4.1). The distribution functions has two parameters. Following Iyengar's paper, we choose $a = 0.5$ and $b = 512$, which is our grain size.

$$P(x) = \frac{ab^a}{x^{a+1}} \qquad \text{for } x \geq b \qquad (4.1)$$

We will come back to the question of optimal file size distribution in Appendix B.

In addition, Quick Fit assumes that the number of allocations and deallocations is approximately equal over time. Taking into account the file size distribution, most of the free extents will be *small*, and thus placed in one of the quick lists. The few larger extents will be placed in the misc list, obviating the need for quick lists corresponding to larger extents, most of which would be empty. If the file size distribution is Gaussian, we can introduce a misc list for sizes *less* than some threshold. In this case, the quick lists are covering the centre of the size distribution. The as yet unallocated space is called *wilderness* (also called *tail* in some literature) and is treated differently. This is the characteristic of the original Quick Fit design, presented by Weinstock [Wei76].

The algorithm maintains an array of pointers to quick lists (Figure 4.2). Free extents below a certain threshold are placed on their respective lists (threshold being 10 grains in this example), and larger extents are placed in a single misc list. The algorithm is separately keeping track of the wilderness which, in this example, starts at 221st grain and is 29 grains in size.

If the number of large free extents becomes significant, a further optimisation is to use several misc lists, ordered by size ranges. This will reduce the number of extents to be searched within each misc list, but will increase the computational complexity of locating the appropriate misc list. This approach is used by [IJC03] in their *Persistent Multiple Free List Fit (PMFLF)* (discussed in more detail in Section 4.2) implementation as shown in Figure 4.6. The design decision is heavily dependent on the expected allocation and deallocation patterns. The ideal start of the misc lists and the size of each misc list range must be determined by the number of extents in each quick and misc list, which should be roughly equal. With only one misc list and the assumption of the Pareto file size distribution, the system can auto-balance the number of quick lists so as to keep the size of the misc list within the reasonable length limit. Auto-balancing is more difficult to maintain when multiple misc lists have to be factored in.

4.2   Analysis of the Allocation Algorithm Used in PMFLF

Before we list the steps of our improved extent location algorithm, we will go through the steps of PMFLF algorithm, pointing out some of the weaknesses and possible improvements. The algorithm distinguishes between requests for small and large extents. An extent request is considered to be large if its size exceeds the last index of the quick list array. Please note that in Figures 4.3 and 4.4, we give the unmodified text as it is presented in [IJC03]. The term "block"

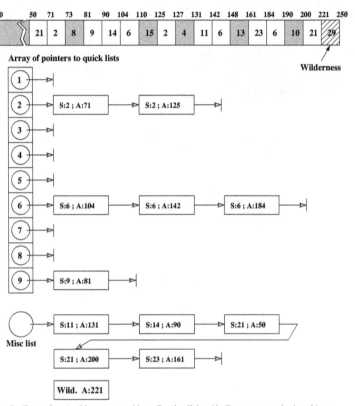

S – Extent size, A – Linear extent address. For simplicity, this diagram uses grain size of 1.
⟶▷ An arrow represents a linked list. Shadowed extents are allocated.

Figure 4.2: The classic QuickFit allocation scheme

in that paper is used in the same sense as the term "extent" in our thesis. The same applies for the term "tail", which is the same as the term "wilderness".

Let us consider Figure 4.3, where PMFLF algorithm for small extent requests is given. Our first observation comes in step 2. By satisfying a request from the wilderness, the algorithm systematically chops up the larger free area into smaller sections, thus increasing the probability that a future large request will not have enough space to be satisfied. The algorithm works for a system where requests are predominantly small and with little variation in size.

The authors justify wilderness allocation by stating that updating wilderness pointer is less costly than splitting due to deferring updates of the wilderness pointer on disk, therefore spreading the cost over several wilderness pointer operations. It is however not given that enough wilderness allocation requests would come during the deference time span. Also, extent splitting cost can be amortised by a careful design of the lazy writer in the Media I/O Layer.

There is another argument against wilderness allocation. Given a

---

For a request for a small block of size s, quick lists are searched in the following fashion:

1. *If the quick list for block of size s is nonempty, allocate the first block from the list. This involves modifying in-memory data structures and a single disk access for modifying the AS field for the block.*

2. *If the previous step fails, satisfy the request from the tail.*

3. *If the previous step fails, examine lists containing larger blocks until a free block is found. This search is conducted in ascending block size order beginning with the list storing blocks belonging to the next larger block class.*

4. *If the previous step fails, coalesce all adjacent free blocks and go to step 1.*

Figure 4.3: PMFLF algorithm for small blocks

sufficiently large number of allocation and deallocation operations, wilderness might no longer be the largest consecutive area of free space. This scenario is illustrated in Figure 4.5.

Step 3 presents the next problem - it does not state splitting criteria. If the wilderness is exhausted and no smaller blocks are present, the algorithm can potentially go through all misc lists, eventually locating a very large block for this small request. As no splitting is specified by the algorithm, the amount of wasted space could be extremely large, if the variation in the size of free extents is large.

Finally, step 4 opens a possibility for an infinite loop if, after the coalescing, there is still no consecutive free space available to satisfy the request.

We now continue to Figure 4.4 and look at which steps are taken to satisfy requests for large extents. In step 4, we again see that wilderness allocation is preferred. The same objections as for the small extent allocation are also applicable here. Step 5 continues

---

The following strategy is used for allocating a large block of size s:

1. *Determine the misc list for block of size s, l_i.*

2. *Allocate the first block in l_i of size t where $s \leq t \leq s + w$ without splitting. (note: w is AWP)*

3. *If the previous step fails, allocate the smallest block on l_i of size t where $s < t$. Split the block into fragments of size s and $t - s$, and return the fragment of size $t - s$ to an appropriate free list.*

4. *If the previous step fails, satisfy the request from the tail.*

5. *If the previous step fails, and $i < n$, search misc lists starting with list l_{i+1} in ascending order. Use the methods of steps 2 and 3 to search each list until an appropriate free block is located.*

6. *If the previous step fails, coalesce all adjacent free blocks and go to step 1.*

Figure 4.4: PMFLF algorithm for large blocks

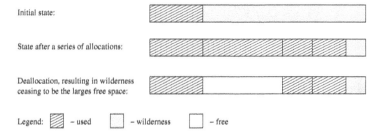

Initial state:

State after a series of allocations:

Deallocation, resulting in wilderness
ceasing to be the larges free space:

Legend: – used   – wilderness   – free

Figure 4.5: Wilderness size reduction

then searching the remaining misc lists if the wilderness space is
exhausted.

4.3 Improved Extent Allocator

Our design is based on the design of PMFLF, with some exten-
sions and is shown in detail in Figure 4.6. All lists are organised
as Skip list structure [Pug89]. First comes an array of pointers to
quick lists. The array is indexed by the size of extents in grains.
This array also contains entries to the empty lists. Thus, given
the grain size, locating an appropriate quick list requires constant
time. We also have a list of ranged misc lists. Extents within each
misc list are sorted first by size and then by address. Search time
for a given extent size in each misc list is $O(\log n)$. The additional
search cost comes from the need to locate the correct misc list.
This cost is $O(\log m)$, where m is the number of misc lists. No tail
pointer is kept, since the unallocated space at the end of the storage is treated as an ordinary extent. In this way we are maintaining
wilderness preservation heuristic (see Section 3.3).

4.3.1 Allocation Hints

The allocation algorithm accepts a size parameter, which tells it
how much space to allocate. In addition two hint parameters –

37

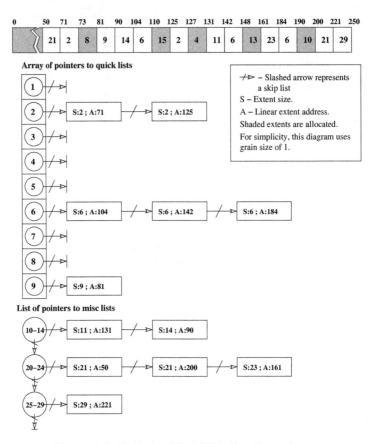

Figure 4.6: Optimised QuickFit allocation scheme

locality and continuity – can be provided. The *locality hint* is a linear address, so that the function attempts to allocate a new extent in the closest possible vicinity after the given hint address. This is useful if additional extents need to be allocated for a growing file. *Continuity hint* instructs the function to perform a more rigorous search for a contiguous extent, rather than returning several fragments. The cost in using continuity hint is an increase in allocation time. Both hints are treated in the best effort manner and no guarantees are given that the allocated extent would satisfy the criteria passed in the hints.

4.3.2 Acceptable Wastage Parameter

One of the parameters used by the extent allocation algorithm is the *acceptable wastage parameter (AWP)*. It determines whether an extent will be split to satisfy a later smaller request or not. If the extent is not split, some storage space is lost to internal fragmentation. The reason behind this parameter is that splitting incurs an additional disk access which is needed to write the header of a newly created extent. As persistent storage is relatively cheap, but slow, high-end applications might prefer to waste some space over using additional time for disk operations. The AWP must, however, be carefully chosen, otherwise too much space can become wasted.

Iyengar et al. [IJC03] do not specify the size of this parameter or how it is calculated. We treat AWP as an absolute value, counted in the number of grains of acceptable wastage. Our experiments offer some insight into this matter (see Section 7.2.4).

4.3.3 New Allocation Algorithm

We now present our modified algorithm for finding one or more extents to satisfy a request of size s. Even though we use ranged misc lists, we will not distinguish between requests for small and large extents, and will not be treating them differently as it is done in PMFLF.

The extents on quick lists are sorted by address. Those belonging to misc lists are first sorted by size and then by address. All size and address calculations are performed in grains.

We maintain two allocator-global variables that are used by the allocation, freeing and coalescing algorithms.

- *Coalesced* flag indicates whether the coalescing algorithm has been performed recently. This flag is set by executing the coalescing algorithm (see Chapter 4.3.4), and cleared on freeing of every extent..

- *Free space* counter holds the current information about the total amount of free space, counted in grains.

The algorithm is divided into three phases. First comes the *Free list location phase*, where it is decided whether a request can be satisfied by allocating exactly one extent, and which free list should be used in that case. Phase two is the *Single-extent allocation phase* and finally there is the *Multi-extent allocation phase*, which is used when no single extent is large enough to satisfy the request. The algorithm returns an error, if it is unable to satisfy the request, or a list of one or more extents, whose total size is greater than or equals to the requested size.

Phase 1: Free list location

1. Adjust the size of a request, converting it from bytes to grains and compensating for the space needed for the extent header. For example, with 512 byte grain size and an 8 byte header, a request for 510 bytes is first adjusted by 8 bytes to 518 bytes and then it is rounded up to the next higher multiple of grain size, which is 1024 bytes in this example. It is then converted to a request for 2 grains of space. By checking the global free space counter, determine whether the request is satisfiable with at least one extent.

2. If the *continuity* hint is given and *coalesced* flag is not set, coalesce all adjacent extents that are currently present on the free lists.

3. For the request of s grains, determine the free list that might contain an extent of t grains, where $t \geq s$. For quick lists, it is enough to consult the entry st index s in the array of quick list pointers. For misc lists, we check that the size of the largest extent in the list is larger than s.

4. If the quick list is empty or no sufficiently large extents are present in the misc list, search through the following lists in sequence, until a list with a suitably large free extent is found.

5. If the last list is reached and no candidate list is still located and *coalesced* flag is not set, coalesce all adjacent extents and go to step 3.

6. If step 5 was executed and still no fitting blocks were located, use multi-extent allocation. Otherwise use single extent allocation.

Phase 2: Single-extent allocation

Phase 1 has found a free list containing a sufficiently large extent of at least t grains in size.

1. If the locality hint is given, find the first extent in the list found in phase 1, whose address is greater than or equal to the one given in the hint. If none is found or when no locality hint is given, use the extent that best fits the provided size.

2. Split the located extent if $AWP + s < t$ and return the remainder to the appropriate free list in the sorted order (*coalesced* flag remains unchanged). Return allocated extent and exit.

Phase 3: Multi-extent allocation

1. Check against the global free space counter that there is enough free space available for the remaining request size and an extent header. If not, free all extents allocated so far, and return an error.

2. Find the list containing the largest available free extent. If the locality hint is given, search the whole list for an extent, whose address is within the shortest distance *after* the address in the hint. Without locality hint use the largest extent. Let the extent's size be t.

41

3. If $s > t$, more extents are still required, so continue to step 4. Otherwise, split the last allocated extent if $AWP + s < t$ and put the remainder to the appropriate free list in the sorted order (*coalesced* flag remains unchanged).

4. Allocate the extent and add it to the return list of allocated extents. If their total size is equal to or greater than the original request size, return the list of allocated extents and exit. Otherwise decrease s by t and repeat step 1.

This algorithm is reasonably fast as the more time-consuming steps, such as coalescing, misc list handling and multi-extent allocation, only have to be taken in the exceptional situations. It tries to maintain spatial locality of the allocated extents if instructed so. The overhead is purely computational and does not incur any additional media accesses.

The algorithm still uses deferred coalescing, except for the continuity hint, when it performs coalescing prior to the location of the extent. The coalesced flag is preserved until any extent is returned to the pool, so that coalescing can be avoided for at least some consecutive allocations. Our algorithm performs coalescing before entering the multi-extent allocation phase. The only real use for the preemptive coalescing is when used in conjunction with the locality hint. In that case preemptive coalescing can increase the probability that a contiguous run of space would be found close to the hinted address. For the coalescing algorithm see Section 4.3.4. The in-depth analysis of effects of coalescing can be found in Sections 7.2.1 and 7.2.6.

Wilderness preservation heuristic [KV85, WJNB95] is observed in that the algorithm always tries to use smaller extents before splitting larger ones, while the largest extent is always used last. For multi-extent allocation phase the algorithm tries to use largest possible extents in an attempt to reduce the overall number of fragments.

The algorithm offers minimal fault tolerance by always keeping the state of the in-memory data structures consistent with the on-disk state. It, for example, reverts to a consistent state if a request cannot be satisfied. We cannot, however, avoid inconsistency, should a system failure occur during the multi-extent allocation phase or

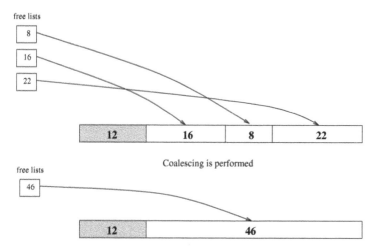

Figure 4.7: Schematic representation of coalescing

when returning the list of allocated extents to the File Link Layer[1] from either of the allocation phases. In those cases, one or more extents are marked as allocated on disk, but never reach the File Link Layer. The responsibility for recovering such lost extents lays on the File Link Layer.

4.3.4 Coalescing Algorithm

In [IJC03] the authors do not explicitly specify the coalescing algorithm. The original design by Weinstock [Wei76] has a specification of coalescing (or collapsing as it is denoted in his work). That algorithm is, however, targeted at main memory allocation and is not suitable for disk space allocation. There, the algorithm rebuilds the free lists from scratch, using the information in the headers and coalescing adjacent blocks as it finds them. This algorithm requires a media access for each retrieved block and is therefore not suitable for slow hard disks.

Below we are going to present a fast coalescing algorithm, which

---

[1]For description see Section 5.2.

43

does not require copying of the in-memory structures and keeps disk accesses to the minimum. A schematic result of running the coalescing algorithm is depicted in Figure 4.7. The size of the ith extent is denoted as S_i, and its address as A_i.

1. Build coalescing list c of all free extents, sorted by address. The extent headers are *moved* from their free lists to c. For this purpose we are using a skip list and insertion sort method. Due to the skip list data structure [Pug89], insertion sort runs efficiently in $O(n \log n)$ time.

2. Traverse c from start to end and coalesce adjacent extents using the following sub-algorithm. Start with i pointing to the first element in c:

   (a) Exit to step 3 if i is the last extent in c. Set j to $i + 1$.

   (b) If $A_j = A_i + S_i$ then j is adjacent to i, in which case:
      - let $S_i = S_i + S_j$;
      - mark extent i as *modified* in memory;
      - if j was the last extent, go to step 3 otherwise let $j = j + 1$ and repeat step 2(b).

   (c) When a non-adjacent extent is found:
      - return extent i to the appropriate free list and update its on-disk header if the extent was modified;
      - let $i = j$;
      - repeat step 2(a).

3. Return extent i to the appropriate free list and update its on-disk header if the extent was modified. Finish.

We use the initial state of the QuickFit structures presented in Figure 4.6 and illustrated the steps taken by the coalescing algorithm in Figure 4.8.

One of the strengths of this algorithm is that no copying of extent headers is performed, thus not requiring any additional space for coalescing.

Disk accesses to update the on-disk extent headers are performed only when necessary – once for each *modified* extent header, after all adjacent headers have been identified. The algorithm does not destroy the on-disk representations of the freed headers.

The algorithm is fault tolerant. Should a system failure occur during its execution, all the on-disk headers will still have valid values. We can use Figure 4.8 for an illustration. Suppose a failure occurs at the point, where extent with address 81 was being coalesced. Then, only extent header with address 50 was ever committed to disk with its new size of 23. During the reconstruction process it will be treated as a single extent, preceding the one with address 81. Thus all extents which headers were not committed before the failure will remain not coalesced.

4.4 Summary

In this chapter we have investigated QuickFit – the existing allocation algorithm, found in PMFLF. We then introduced a wide range of modifications which will improve the efficiency of the allocator, while reducing the complexity of design. In the next chapters we continue with the design of a system, which incorporates our improved allocator. We will the implement and test our design to verify the positive effect of our modifications.

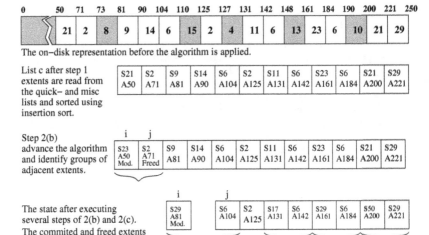

The on-disk representation before the algorithm is applied.

List c after step 1
extents are read from
the quick- and misc
lists and sorted using
insertion sort.

Step 2(b)
advance the algorithm
and identify groups of
adjacent extents.

The state after executing
several steps of 2(b) and 2(c).
The commited and freed extents
are removed from the list.

After coalescing is complete, the free lists are rebuilt and the on-disk state has this layout:

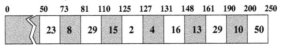

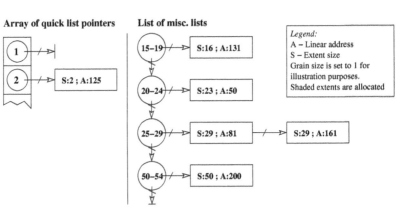

Figure 4.8: The steps of the coalescing algorithm

46

Chapter 5

Design

5.1 System Overview

In this chapter we give a short presentation of the system's parameters. In the next chapter each component is described in more detail.

Design goals of the Extent-Based Disk Allocator are:

- It should be implementable and efficient on hard disks, with support for Linear Block Addressing (LBA). Most, if not all, modern hard drives hide the physical details of the media, providing the operating system with a linear addressing interface.

- We target high-end systems with fast data transfer rates and processing times to absorb the expected housekeeping overhead.

- The system would be used in the environments where file size is fairly homogeneous. In such an environment the fragmentation would have least impact on the allocator performance.

We are going to use a layered model, shown in Figure 5.1, which also lists functions, belonging to each layer. Following sections describe the layers in more detail.

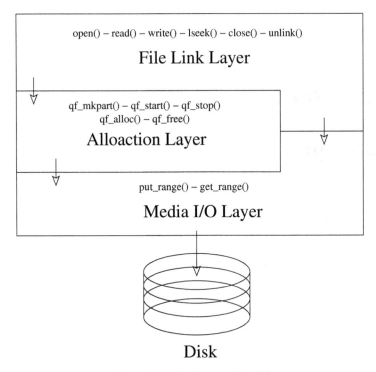

Figure 5.1: The layered model

5.2 File Link Layer

The *File Link Layer* maintains the data structures responsible for associating (linking) files with their corresponding extent(s). It receives the usual file system calls and communicates with the intended subsystems. Read operations communicate directly to the Media I/O Layer. Likewise write requests, unless they require growing of a file, in which case the Allocation Layer is first invoked, and then the extent obtained from the allocation is filled with data and sent for I/O. File creation and deletion always go through the Allocation Layer.

48

File Link Layer accepts *open()*, *read()*, *write()*, *lseek()*, *close()* and *un-link()* requests. They are typically invoked from the corresponding system calls, after routing through the Virtual File System (VFS) layer[1].

We describe these functions here for the purpose of completeness and from the allocator's point of view. We are only going to implement the allocator and test it by means of simulation. The simulation driver will only have the rudimentary functionality of *open()* and *unlink()* functions, which correspond to the events present in the allocation trace. For a complete picture of a file system, the reader is referred to [Tan01].

5.2.1 open()

open() has two sub-functions.

- If a file does not exist, *open()* initialises bookkeeping structures, internal to the File Link Layer. In some cases, the size of the file to be created is known beforehand, as for example when we wish to copy a file. In such situation a special variant of *open()* function, which accepts size as one of its parameters, can be used. This variant would beforehand allocate the extents needed to store the specified amount of data. This is in effect what is done by the simulation driver in response to the allocation operation command of the trace.

- If a file already exists, the File Link Layer creates an inode in memory and associates it with the file's on-disk representation. An inode contains addresses of the extents associated with the file, a read/write permissions field, a file pointer to the next I/O operation and any additional attributes that might be needed for housekeeping purposes. In this simulation the inode is limited to holding a unique file ID number and a list of allocated extents, associated with that file.

5.2.2 write()

write() is the most complex function. If enough space is allocated

---
[1]Not discussed in this thesis

49

for the data to be stored (e.g.: file pointer points to the middle of the file), then we see which portions of the extents needs to be updated and send corresponding requests to the Media I/O Layer. If all or some of the data are targeted to the area outside the extents already allocated, then an extent of a certain size is requested from the Allocation Layer. It should be noted here that Allocation Layer may return more than one extent if it does not manage to find a contiguous region. The returned extent is linked with the file and its address along with the data to be written is sent to the I/O Layer.

It is File Link Layer's responsibility to determine the size of the extent to be allocated, with regard to possible overbooking of space, if the file is known to be a growing one. For example, if a file was extended more than certain number of times during some period of time, such a file is marked as "growing". The extents of growing files could then be allocated aggressively, meaning more space is allocated for such a file than initially requested. This strategy intends to lessen file fragmentation of growing files as storage space will already be allocated for a certain number of subsequent writes. The same strategy can be applied to the first write operation of any file in case the newly-created file will be a growing one. When a file stops growing, then it can be truncated to free the unused overbooked space. This strategy is used to some degree in Linux' *ext2fs*.

None of this advanced functionality will be implemented for our simulation as it does not affect the performance of the allocator itself. The allocator will only provide an implementation of *locality* and *continuity* hints, which can potentially be used by an advanced implementation of the *write()* function in some future study, which would aim at investigating the performance of a *file system* using our allocator.

5.2.3 read()

The task of *read()* is rather simple. It finds which extent holds the desired data by going through the size attributes of the extents that comprise the file. It then sends extent address, offset into the extent, data length and target buffer to the Media I/O Layer. As we do not operate with payload data in our simulation, this function does not need to be implemented.

5.2.4 lseek()

lseek() function updates the current file offset in a file's inode, which indicates where the next read or write operation will take place. No changes to the allocation structures are made. Neither this function will be implemented for the simulation.

5.2.5 close()

close() marks a file's control record as closed and removes it from the list of the open inodes. It can then instruct Media I/O Layer to flush its cache of modified information. If the file was marked as growing and its allocation was performed in an overbooking manner *close()* can in addition truncate the file and return the remainder to the Allocation Layer. The *close()* function will not be implemented in the simulator.

5.2.6 unlink()

unlink() instructs the Allocation Layer to free the extents associated with the file, and then removes the internal structures representing the file. It is the Allocation Layer's responsibility to call the Media I/O Layer to update the extents' headers.

If a file is still opened when *unlink()* is called, the function should fail. It is the simplest solution and the one used in Microsoft Windows. Alternatively we could mark the file as deleted, but defer the actual deletion until the last reference to the file is closed. This approach is used in various UNIX flavours, but is more difficult to implement.

As there are no *open* or *close* operations in the trace, *unlink()* just deallocates extents.

51

5.3 Allocation Layer

The *Allocation Layer* is responsible for keeping track of the free extents and performing the housekeeping operations on them, such as splitting and coalescing. Allocation Layer services the requests from File Link Layer and returns a list of one or more free extents to it.

Allocation Layer has two functions, which execute all the requests from the File Link Layer, based on the supplied parameters. These functions are *qf_alloc()* and *qf_free()*. In addition, *qf_start()* and *qf_stop()* are called during system start-up and shut-down. A partition is created using function *qf_mkpart()*.

5.3.1 qf_mkpart()

qf_mkpart() is responsible for creating and initialising a partition. It reserves a grain-sized extent for internal data – a *superblock*, which is used by *qf_start()* and *qf_stop()*. This includes the information about the first extent containing saved state, a flag indicating the validity of the saved state and a flag saying whether the partition was unmounted cleanly.

As our simulator does not support stopping and restarting of the trace execution, the implementation of *qf_mkpart()* will only include the initialisation of the in-memory representation of a partition. This means that some of the functionality of *qf_start()* (described next) and *qf_mkpart()* is merged.

5.3.2 qf_start()

qf_start() is the function that would typically be called at file system mount. It first tries to restore the free lists from the data saved during the shut-down process and then clears the on-disk flag which is marking the saved data as valid. This is done so that an eventual crash at a later point would lead to data reconstruction.

If the saved data are not initially marked as valid, *qf_start()* reconstructs the free lists by traversing all the extents on the hard disk. It starts with the first extent header of the partition. If the AS field indicates that the extent is free, it is added to the appropriate free list, based on its size. Then the next extent is located by adding size value of the current extent to the current extent address. This continues until the end of the partition is reached.

Finally, the extents used for the restoration space are themselves put into the free list. The system state is then changed to *mounted*.

We will not be implementing this function in our simulation as we leave it to future work to analyse the effects of saving the allocator's state to disk.

5.3.3 qf_stop()

The task of *qf_stop()* is to save the state of the allocator before a file system is unmounted. The space for the saved state is allocated by the allocator itself, and the address of the first extent is stored in the superblock extent reserved by *qf_mkpart()*. If there is not enough free space, the allocator cannot save its state and will have to go through a slower reconstruction process during the startup.

The function first marks the saved state to be read by *qf_start()* as invalid. It then writes extent headers from all free lists to the disk. Finally the saved state is marked as valid. This way we ensure that the free lists are reconstructed from the saved state only if they were completely committed to disk. A failure, preventing a quick reconstruction of free lists can arise if there is not enough hard disk space to write all the header information or if the system crashes due to, for example, a power failure during the commit phase.

As the last step, the system state is changed to *unmounted* to indicate that all on-disk extent headers are in a consistent state. This happens even if the function was unable to save the restoration data.

We will not be implementing *qf_stop()* in our simulator.

5.3.4 qf_alloc()

qf_alloc() satisfies the allocation requests. It uses a variation of the Quick Fit algorithm as described in Section 4.3.3 and the coalescing algorithm described in Section 4.3.4.

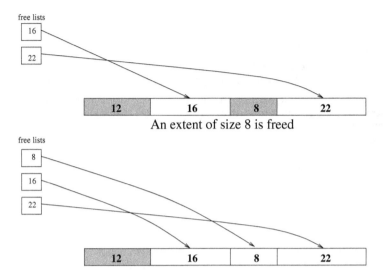

Figure 5.2: A schematic representation of extent freeing

5.3.5 qf_free()

qf_free() is supplied with a list of extents that are to be freed. The function locates an appropriate free list for each extent and inserts the extent into it, observing sorting criteria. The AS field of the on-disk header is cleared through the Media I/O Layer. The allocator-global *coalesced* flag (see Section 4.3.3) is cleared for the benefit of the allocation algorithm. Note that the extents are not coalesced at this point, which is schematically illustrated in Figure 5.2.

5.4 Media I/O Layer

The *Media I/O Layer* receives requests from the upper layers and writes and reads extents or their parts from the hard disk. Typically it would interact with the buffer cache of the operating system. If buffer cache is not available, it can include a variation of a *lazy writer* to allow grouping of write operations by performing them in bursts.

All requests to the layer are in the form of *extent address, offset into extent, data length and data pointer* tuple. As extents can be very large, it is not practical to perform writes on a whole extent. A minimum disk transaction size must still be observed, so no request can be smaller than one sector in size.

The layer contains two functions: *get_range()* and *put_range()*. Though we will describe much of the functionality of a complete version, the implementation is kept as simple as possible due to the goals of our allocator simulation.

5.4.1 get_range()

get_range() reads the requested amount of bytes from the disk and places the data in the provided buffer. Data are read in an aligned manner in complete grains to guarantee sector alignment. The requested subset of data is then copied to the target buffer and returned to the calling layer. This function will not be needed for the purpose of the simulation as our version of the allocator only performs write operations.

5.4.2 put_range()

put_range(), just like *get_range()* performs I/O transaction in integral numbers of grains. It means that, for example, to write an extent header, a total of 512 bytes need to be written to the disk. Another implication is that if only a portion of the grain is to be modified, then the complete grain has to be read from the disk, modified in memory and then written back. In some situations, when old content of the grain is unimportant, the read operation can be omitted. To signal this, *put_range()* accepts an extra parameter, telling it whether the write operation will be performed in a destructive manner. The destructive writing is used, for example, when the Allocation Layer updates the on-disk extent headers because the contents of the extents is meaningless prior to allocation and is no longer needed after freeing.

A form of a "lazy writer" can also belong to this function, if the underlying operating system does not implement a buffer cache.

In [IJC03] the authors describes it as *Optimised Batch Allocation (OBA)*. They, however, logically place this mechanism at the Allocation Layer level. Several allocation requests are accumulated, but no extent assignments are performed. After a certain period of time all free extents in the lists are combined into a single list, sorted by size and all the backlogged allocations are executed from this list against a single sorted list of free extents. This effectively degrades Quick Fit algorithm to a linear Best Fit implementation.

For the purpose of this simulation *put_range()* will be kept as simple as possible. We do not perform any writing at all, but instead count the number of disk accesses that would have been performed.

5.5 Summary

In this chapter we introduced the design for our improved allocator and a surrounding file system. As the primary goal of this thesis is the design and evaluation of an allocator, we kept the discussion of the file system functionality to the minimum, concentrating on those functions, which will be implemented in the simulation driver. In the next chapter we present implementation detail for each function of the allocator and the simulation driver, using the outlined design presented in this chapter.

Chapter 6

Implementation

In this chapter we describe the implementation of our allocator. The reader is referred to Appendix B for the presentation of the properties of the allocation trace in use. The source code listings are available in Appendix C. The specifics of the trace will dictate some of the implementation characteristics of our allocator.

We will start with an overview of the system and a presentation of once central data structure, used throughout the entire simulator – Skip Lists. We will then continue with describing data structures and implementation details of each part of the allocator.

6.1 Overview

Based on the goals of our simulation we consider it sufficient to implement a fully-functional extent management part of the allocator with some rudimentary interfacing to the Media I/O layer. The implementation of the simulator follows the general layered layout we presented in Chapter 5.1.

The File Link layer is represented by the trace driver. Because we do not have any data to be stored in the files, it is sufficient for the trace driver to perform a series of *qf_alloc()* and *qf_free()* calls. The driver also initialises the allocator with a certain amount of free space through a call to *qf_mkpart()* function.

As the trace is executed in one continuous operation, we do not need to implement the functionality of the *qf_start()* and *qf_stop()*

functions. The impact of stopping the execution on the placement decisions after a restore is left for future work.

The allocation and deallocation operations that the allocator is requested to perform, always result in one type of disk write operations – extent header updates. As disks vary in size and performance parameters, it is more accurate and reproducible for our allocator to count the number of write requests that have to be performed as a result of a trace operation. The Media I/O layer therefore implements only a rudimentary *put_range()* function, which increments a write operation counter.

We use *Skip lists* [Pug89] to organise all internal data structures of both the simulation driver and the allocator itself. Skip lists have several desirable properties, comparable to other data structures, such as balanced binary search trees. At the same times they are easy to implement and maintain. The reader is referred to Appendix C.2.2 for the implementation details.

6.2 Simulation Driver Implementation

6.2.1 Data Structures

The trace driver keeps track of the individual "files" in the `sim_file` structure. It contains a copy of the *create* trace event, which holds the information about the file size and the file's ID number. The `sim_file` structure also contains a pointer to a skip list of allocated extents, associated with this file. This structure corresponds to the inode structure of a File Link Layer.

```
1  // From storage_types.h:
2  #define OP_CREATE    1
3  #define OP_DELETE    2
4  #define FL_REPLACED 16
5  #define FL_DELMOD   32
6
7  struct alloc_trace {
8    unsigned int    file_id;
9    unsigned int    size;     //set to 0 if operation is "delete"
10   unsigned char   flags;    //Contains OP_ and FL_ flags
11 } __attribute__((packed));
12
```

```
13  //From simalloc.h:
14  struct sim_file{
15    struct alloc_trace at;
16    struct skip_list *ext;
17  };
```

The Memory Statistics Module

As part of the simulation, the driver gathers statistics about memory consumption by the allocator and the driver itself. For this purpose we have written wrapper functions for *malloc()* and *free()*, called *stat_malloc()* and *stat_free()*. In addition to the usual parameters accepted by the underlying functions, the wrapper functions take in a parameter of memstat_t type (shown below), which tells the wrapper function which part of the program issued the call:

```
1  typedef enum {
2    MEM_IGNORE,     //All skip lists are traced by default. This class
3                    //is used if we want to disable tracing.
4    MEM_MLL,        //The list of misc lists
5    MEM_QLISTS,     //Quick lists
6    MEM_MLISTS,     //Misc lists
7    MEM_EXTENT,     //In-memory extent headers
8    MEM_COAL,       //Coalescing master list
9  } memstat_t;
```

The module keeps an array of meminfo structures, containing a structure for each of the categories in the memstat_t type.

```
1  struct meminfo{
2    uint64_t running;
3    uint64_t max;
4    uint64_t total;
5    FILE *malloc_file;
6    FILE *free_file;
7  };
```

All pointers to allocated memory, along with their sizes are kept in a dedicated skip list, which is ordered by memory address values.

59

6.2.2 Implementation Details

The trace driver consists of three central functions – *trc_driver()*, *create_file()* and *delete_file()*.

First, the *main()* function initialises all the parts of the simulator, memory statistics module (described later) and the media I/O interface. It also creates a new partition with the user-provided size and AWP values by calling the *qf_mkpart()* function. Finally *trc_driver()* function is called.

trc_driver() is a loop which reads an event from the trace and calls either *create_file()* or *delete_file()* depending on the operation stored in the trace's `flags` field. The function also collects statistics about the maximum amount of disk space that would be needed at any given time.

The *create_file()* function creates a new `sim_file` object and calls *qf_alloc()* to request the extents for this file. It then stores the structure in a skip list of active files, which is sorted by the file ID number.

The *delete_file()* function locates and removes a file with the given ID number from the list of active files. The extents, which belonged to that file are then returned to the free pool by calling *qf_free()* function. Finally, the memory occupied by the `sim_file` structure is freed.

The Memory Statistics Module

The *stat_malloc()* function first passes the call to the usual *malloc()*. It then creates an entry consisting of the returned address and the size and stores that entry in a skip list. The total and the maximum memory consumption by the provided category is calculated and stored in the appropriate entry of the `meminfo` structure. If writing of statistics to file is enables, the current memory consumption by the particular category is written to disk.

The *stat_free()* retrieves the memory node information from the skip list, using the provided address as a key. The sizes values of the provided category are updated and an eventual write out of the new memory consumption to disk is performed. It then calls the standard *free()* to free the memory referenced by the pointer.

6.3 Allocator Implementation

6.3.1 Data Structures

The central structure of the allocator is the `qf_allocator` structure. It holds an array of skip lists, representing the quick lists of the algorithm. All free lists originate in this structure. The Quick lists are implemented an array of skip lists, `ql`. The pointers to the misc lists are organised in the `mll` skip list – a list of misc lists. The boolean `coalesced` flag corresponds to the one mentioned in the algorithm and determines if the coalescing procedure should be run. Finally, the `free` member holds a continuously updated information about the amount of space available for allocation, which is counted in grains.

Each misc list is rooted in `misc_list` structure, which contains a skip list of free extents assigned to the misc list and the starting value of the misc list size range. The pointers to the instances of this structure are stored in the nodes of `mll` skip list of the `qf_allocator` structure.

All the free lists hold pointers to the `extent` structure at their nodes. The structure describes and extent by its size and its address.

At this point we must also note that all addresses and sizes use a user-defined type `asize_t`, which is 64 bits in size in the current implementation, but can easily adjusted for other purposes. All addresses and sizes used internally in the allocator are counted in grains.

```
1  //From common.h;
2  typedef enum {
3      FALSE,
4      TRUE,
5  } bool_t;
6
7  typedef uint64_t asize_t; // Address size in grains
8
9  struct extent{
10     asize_t        size;
11     asize_t        address;
12 };
13
```

61

```
14  //From allocator.h:
15  struct misc_list{
16    asize_t            range_idx;
17    struct skip_list extents;
18  };
19
20  struct qf_allocator{
21    struct skip_list ql[NUM_QUICK_LISTS];
22    struct skip_list mll;
23    bool_t             coalesced;
24    asize_t            free;        // Number of free grains
25  };
```

6.3.2   Implementation Details

The implementation of the allocator closely followed our proposed
design of Section 5.3 as well as the algorithms described in Sections 4.3.3 and 4.3.4. The implementation is modular and uses
many helper functions to perform frequent or common tasks, such
as removing an extent from a free list or splitting an extent. Below
we will describe some of the central parts of the allocator implementation.

Initialisation

The allocator is initialised in function *qf_mkpart()*. The function
first initialises the qf_allocator structure and all its permanent
skip lists. It then proceeds to creating a new extent with the provided size and a starting address of 0. The size of a new virtual
partition provided to the function is in bytes, so it is converted to
grains before the *wilderness* extent is created. Finally the extent is
stored in an appropriate free list by a call to the general *store_ext()*
function.

Allocation

The implementation of function *qf_alloc()* and its helper functions
closely follows the allocation algorithm described in Section 4.3.3.
The function is provided with a request for desired size in bytes,

along with a continuity hint and a locality hint. The locality hint is a grain (or LBA) based address, so *qf_alloc()* does not need to convert it. The size value is, on the other hand, adjusted as described in the algorithm, taking into account the size required to store the extent header.

A preliminary check is then made to ensure that the request can be satisfied at all. It is easier to perform than catching failure conditions in several different helper functions, which are called during the allocation process.

The function then takes the steps described in the allocation algorithm, calling helper functions to perform an eventual coalescing and branching off to a single-extent or a multi-extent allocation.

Single-extent Allocation

The function for single extent allocation, *single_alloc()*, locates a suitable extent in the provided candidate free list and returns it as the only node of the provided skip list. We use a skip list for both single-extent and multi-extent allocation to provide a uniform interface to the File Link Layer.

The function is provided in the desired size in grains, as calculated by the *qf_alloc()* function.

Depending on the type of the candidate free list, either *find_ext_ql()* or *find_ext_ml()* helper functions is called. The distinction is made because of the different search criteria for the two types of the lists.

- *find_ext_ql()* returns the first extent on the quick list if no locality hint is given. With locality hint, it performs a skip list search, finding an extent which address is greater than or equal to the provided locality address.

- *find_ext_ml()* is more complex. Without locality hint, it distinguishes between the cases of being invoked from *multi_alloc()* and *single_alloc()*. In the first case it simply returns the last extent on the misc list, which is, by sorting invariant, is the largest one. In the latter case, is searches the skip list for any extent which size is greater than or equal to the provided size parameter. With the locality hint, *find_ext_ml()* acts the same, independently from where it was called. It first uses skip list

63

search to quickly locate the first extent of a suitable size and address. It then proceeds traversing the skip list node for node, trying to find an even better locality match at the cost of returning a larger extent than requested.

Before returning the located extent, a final comparison is made to ensure that the extent is not too large. If it is larger than the boundary of the AWP parameter, the extent is split, using a helper function.

Multi-extent Allocation

The function *multi_alloc()* is also written to closely follow the proposed algorithm.

The size parameter, received by the function is in bytes, because we cannot determine beforehand how many extents will be needed to satisfy the request and the on-disk space consumed by each extent has to be taken into account on the fly.

The whole function is a single do...while loop, which allocates individual extents in a fashion, similar to the single-extent allocation method, until the total size of the allocated extents is equal to or greater than the provided size. The last extent might need splitting if it exceeds the boundaries set by AWP. The body of the loop is divided into three distinct phases.

In the first phase we check if there are enough grains to accommodate the remaining bytes and a header. If we are out of disk space, the return list must be cleared and deleted as some extents might have been already allocated prior to the failure.

In the second phase we locate a candidate free list with the largest possible extent. The candidate list can either be a quick- or a misc list. We then use either *find_ext_ql()* or *find_ext_ml()* to retrieve and extent of desired size and location. These functions were described in the previous, Single-extent Allocation, section.

In the third phase we perform size comparisons to see if more extents are needed. In case the extent is last one, we additionally check if splitting needs to be done. Finally, the allocated extents are added to the provided skip list.

Deleting and Storing of the Extents

The extents are removed from their free lists by a call to *delete_ext()* function. This function first removes the extent from its skip list and then checks if it was the last extent on a misc list, in which case the misc list itself is deleted from the list of misc lists. The commit parameter is used to determine whether the changes should be written to disk. We do not want to do an excessive header update if an extent splitting is about to occur, because the splitting function will need to update the extent header anyway. The on-disk headers are neither updated if the extents are removed for the purpose of coalescing.

The function *store_ext()* is responsible for placing a newly-freed extent in an appropriate free list, creating a new misc list if it is needed. In the end the function makes an update of the on-disk header. The boolean parameter commit governs that action. It is kept for the benefit of the coalescing function to avoid an extra disk access if an extent is returned to a free list without being modified.

Both functions adjust the free member of the qf_allocator structure, thus keeping the free space counter up to date.

Freeing

When a file is deleted, *qf_free()* function is called with the return list of extents as its parameter. The function goes through the list, moving the extents from it to the appropriate free lists. In the end the return list itself is deleted.

The *qf_free()* function can also be called inside the allocator from *multi_alloc()*, if that function fails to acquire enough extents to satisfy a request and must abort the allocation process.

Splitting

Both *single_alloc()* and *multi_alloc()* call *split_ext()* function to trim down the provided extent to a new size and write that size to the on-disk header. The remainder is placed in an appropriate free list by a call to *store_ext()* function.

Coalescing

The flow of the *coalesce()* function follows closely the algorithm provided in Chapter 4.3.4. We use a skip list, which we call a `clist` to created an address-sorted sequence of all extents on the free lists. The sorting process is basically an implementation of an insertion sort algorithm. The sorting time is, however, $O(n \log n)$, thanks to the properties of the skip lists. The on-disk headers of the extents are not touched during this phase, so an eventual failure will not affect the integrity of the system.

Next we coalesce the extents and move them to the appropriate free lists. We instruct th *store_ext()* function to update the on-disk header of the returned extent only in case it was modified by being merged with other extents.

We use a one-pass implementation of the algorithm. It is safe to use as long as we do not clear the on-disk headers of the merged-in extents. If the obsoleted extent headers are to be cleared, we need a more time consuming two-pass implementation to ensure fault-tolerance, marking the extents as freed and modified in the first pass, while using the second pass to write out modified extents *before* the freed ones are cleared. That way, if a crash occurs during the second pass, the integrity of the on-disk headers would be preserved.

Finally the `coalesced` flag of the `qf_allocator` structure is set and the now empty `clist` is deleted.

Header updating

All header updates are executed through functions *read_hdr()* and *write_hdr()*. In the current implementation, *read_hdr()* is never used by the allocator and has therefore only a rudimentary call to the Media I/O Layer. The *write_hdr()* function is fully implemented. It first scrambles the size and the allocation status values as shown in Figure 3.1 in Chapter 3.2. It then call the *put_range()* function of the Media I/O Layer to commit the header in a destructive way.

66

6.4 Media I/O Layer Implementation Details

The Media I/O Layer's two interface functions are *put_range()* and *get_range()*. Both functions are implemented in a rudimentary fashion, updating the write and read counters respectively.

The *put_range()* function, has the parameters describing the disk address and the size of the data to be written and a pointer to the data itself. In addition, it has a boolean `destructive` flag. If set, the function will not preserve the remaining contents of a grain if only a portion of that grain need to be modified. This a normal case for the allocator – when an extent is allocated, it does not yet have any payload, so overwriting the bytes after the header is not dangerous. Similarly, when an extent is freed, its payload is no longer needed and can be destroyed.

As the *get_range()* function is never called either directly or through the *put_range()* function, its counter will always remain zero in our simulator.

6.5 Summary

In this chapter we presented the implementation of the allocator, based on our improved design, along with the simulation driver and statistics collection modules, which we will use to evaluate our implementation in the next chapter. Our implementation is modular, simple and is easy to maintain. Whereas XFS claims to use approximately 50000 lines of C code [SDH+96], our implementation uses 2200 lines for the allocator and the supporting system. Even if the File Link and Media I/O layers were fully implemented, we doubt that the complete system would have used more than 20000 lines of code.

This implementation will be thoroughly evaluated using a wide variety of tests presented in the next chapter.

Chapter 7

Evaluation

7.1 Evaluation Parameters

Based on the trace characteristics described in the previous chapter, we can now perform the evaluation of our allocator's performance. We start by describing the adjustable parameters of the allocator, then continue to presenting the properties of the allocator that we wish to evaluate. We finish this chapter with the presentation of the evaluation results.

7.1.1 Adjustable Parameters

The allocator has four degrees of freedom, which can be modified to adjust its performance:

- grain size;
- the size of the partition;
- acceptable wastage parameter (AWP) value and
- the activation of the coalescing code.

We use a constant grain size and set it to the hard disk sector size value of 512 bytes. We will now look at each of the remaining parameters and define the values to be used with the simulation.

The Size of the Partition

The partition size value is a parameter that affects the performance of the allocator in the strongest way. Given enough space, all requests from the trace can be satisfied by allocating new extents one after another. This way, the simulation will not be affected by the other two parameters.

For this simulation we define four partition size classes. All sizes are relative to the maximum number of bytes of disk space requested by the simulation driver at any given time – the *peak load* of the trace. When describing the simulations we will always state which partition class was used.

The peak load of our trace, adjusted for header size and minimum internal fragmentation wastage is 9683949 grains or **4728.49MB**. This value was obtained by running the simulator with the *estimated*[1] maximum allocated bytes value, as reported by the trace generation program and AWP set to zero.

The partition size classes and their sizes in megabytes are:

Huge partition size set to the double of the peak load or **9458MB**.

> This partition class can be seen as a "generous corporate company" class, where a system administrator always has resources to install additional hard disks long before they are needed.

Large partition is 10% larger than required by the trace. It is **5201MB** in our simulation.

> This class represents a "good administrator", who never lets the system run out of space completely, but at the same time is not willing to waste money to buy new hard disks before they are needed.

Medium partition provides 1% more space than the maximum trace load. It is **4776MB** in our simulation.

> This class is for a "lazy administrator", who checks on the system once a month to see if it is still running and installing

---

[1]The estimation process of the trace generator does not have access to the deletion time of a file until the complete log is parsed. It therefore treats all not replaced files as though they live until the end of the simulation, thus producing a large overestimation. See output from trace generator in Appendix D.1.2

the new disk capacity at the last possible moment. Or maybe the said administrator never gets the funding he asks about?

Minimum partition has only enough space to satisfy the peak load, rounded up to the nearest megabyte. It is **4729MB** in our simulation.

This is a scenario, where a company decided that they do not need an administrator at all, and after firing him, they promptly forget about the system needs and allow it run completely dry.

The partition size is controlled at run time by -p parameter passed to the simulator program.

Acceptable Wastage Parameter

AWP has the second strongest influence on the space utilisation as it consciously increases the internal fragmentation. Most of the tests will be run with no wastage, that is AWP set to zero. Only the tests designed to evaluate the impact of AWP on system utilisation will change AWP to other values. We will however never use AWP that is greater than 18 grains due to reasons described in Section 7.2.4.

AWP is set during run time by the -w parameter. If omitted, zero AWP is assumed.

Coalescing Off Parameter

The presence of coalescing is the last parameter of our allocator, which can be changed. Coalescing can be considered as one of the more costly operations, both in terms of computational demands and the number of disk accesses. We shall investigate this by turning the coalescing procedure off while keeping other parameters unchanged and observe the effects.

Coalescing can be turned off at run time bu supplying the -nc parameter on the simulator's command line.

7.1.2 Overview of Measurements

There are many aspects of the allocator that can be measured. We decided to perform measurements which show the effects of the above-mentioned parameters in the clearest manner. These measurements are:

- Memory consumption of the various allocator categories as the simulation is progressing.

- The allocator's computational overhead, measured in the time needed to complete the simulation for each partition class.

- The number of write operations as a function of initial free space.

- Impact of AWP on the number of write operations when the partition size and coalescing state are held constant.

- Internal fragmentation as a function of trace execution progression.

- Internal fragmentation at peak allocation load.

- File fragmentation as a correlation between the number of extents allocated and the number of files in the trace.

- The efficiency of the coalescing algorithm, counting further:

    - the number of calls to the coalescing function;
    - the number of extents merged for each call
    - coalescings resulting in single-extent allocations;
    - coalescings, where multi-extent allocation was still needed and
    - coalescings avoided due to setting of the *coalesced* status flag (see Section 4.3.4).

- The impact of coalescing in the near-exhaustion case on the file fragmentation and the number of write operations.

- The state of the free disk space pool as the simulation progresses.

In the next section we will describe each test in more detail and present the evaluation results.

7.2   Test Results

This section covers the evaluation tests performed to examine the efficiency of our allocator. For each test we first describe its purpose, then present its parameters and finally give the results along with a short analyses.

All tests were run on Cygwin_NT 5.1 with a 3,2GHz Pentium 4HT CPU and one gigabyte of physical memory.

7.2.1   Memory Usage

In this test we examine the allocator's memory consumption. We are interested in both the final state and the development throughout the simulation run. For this purpose, we instruct the memory module to dump the running consumption of memory by various part of the simulation to files as memory allocations and frees occur.

For this test we are going to run the simulation with *Large* partition size class, AWP set to 0 and coalescing enabled. Large partition size is chosen because the simulation is expected to make use of all its components, without placing excessive stress on them.

We can expect a small variation in memory load from test run to test run, due to the random nature of skip list node allocation. The results presented here are from one representative test run.

When collecting data about the memory load, we take note at what time during the execution a particular measurement was taken. In this case, we measure the time in *memory management events*, where an event counter is advanced during each call to *stat_malloc()* or *stat_free()*, independent of which allocator component initiated the call. That way we can easily consolidate data collected from various parts of the allocator into combined graphs.

Moreover, we *must* use memory management events, as there is no one-to-one correlation between memory usage events and the events in the trace. For example, a coalescing causes several thousand memory events in free lists, extent headers and the coalescing list categories. A coalescing is, however, initiated by *one* trace event. If trace events were used, all the dynamics of memory usage

73

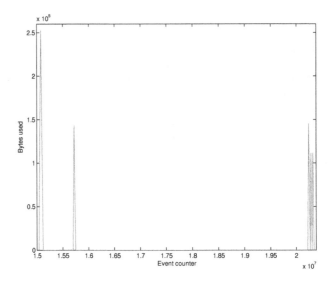

Figure 7.1: Memory usage for coalescing

would have been lost. Therefore, all memory usage graphs have these *memory management events* along their X-axis.

Tracking memory consumption gives us an additional bonus – we can indirectly visualise the inner workings of the allocator as it executes the trace and point out the various stages of the allocation process. This feature of the memory consumption analysis is so useful, that we will be referring to these graphs in the later test of the specific allocator sub-systems.

After approximately half way through trace execution the total amount of memory consumed by the allocator reaches a steady state, where the number of memory allocations and deallocations is approximately equal.

74

Coalescing List

On Figure 7.1 we can see five spikes, three of which come back-to-back at the right-hand-side of the graph. The number of spikes tells us that coalescing was performed five times, while the height of the spikes reflects the total number of extents that had to be sorted and coalesced. In the worst case, the coalescing list consumed 25000 bytes. However large this number seems, we must remember that the free lists are emptied during the coalescing and consume less memory. We shall see it in the correlation analysis.

The fact that the subsequent coalescings used about half as much space can be explained by a supposition that fewer free extents managed to accumulate since the previous one. Here we must also draw attention to the fact that the first coalescing occurred more than half way through the trace execution, as it can be seen from the event counter[2]. Free disjoint extents had therefore much longer time to accumulate before the first coalescing took place.

We will see this graph again when looking at the memory usage correlation between various parts of the allocator.

List of Misc Lists

Another interesting part of the allocator, which consumes little memory, but greatly reflects the flow of the simulation, is the list of misc lists.

As we recall, misc lists are themselves stored on a dynamically adjusted list. When a misc list becomes empty, it is deleted and removed from the list of misc lists. From Figure 7.2 we can see that this tactic pays off as the size of the list does decrease during some parts in the middle of the simulation.

---

[2]Though there is no one-to-one correlation between file and memory allocation and deallocation events, the majority of file allocation will result in one memory operation, when an extent is removed from a quick list without splitting. Likewise, the majority of file freeing will result in one memory operation, when one extent is moved to its designated free list. The exceptions, where additional memory operations are required are not numerous. Such operations are: 1) multi-extent allocation and freeing; 2) misc list administration, resulting in manipulation of the list of misc lists; 3) splittings and 4) coalescing. We can therefore read from the memory consumption graphs an *approximate* position of the file event trace execution progression.

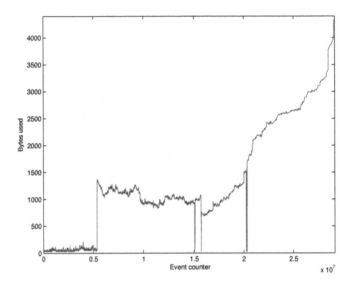

Figure 7.2: Memory usage by the list of misc lists

The graph displays several distinctive features. We shall now look at each of them.

Between events $5.37 \cdot 10^6$ and $5.39 \cdot 10^6$ we observe a sudden increase in the memory consumed by the list of misc lists. This is magnified in Figure 7.3. This can happen during a sequence of extent allocations, where after each splitting the free portion of an extent would have such an inconvenient size that it has to be placed on its own misc list. This supposition is supported by the fact that the load on the list decreases steadily and relatively fast after that, meaning that many of the spread-sized extents came in use short time after the burst.

We observe that prior to the burst the majority of splittings resulted in new extents either being placed on the same misc lists or moved to the quick lists. This will be more obvious when we examine the correlation graph later in this chapter.

The next interesting group of events is the effect of coalescing on

76

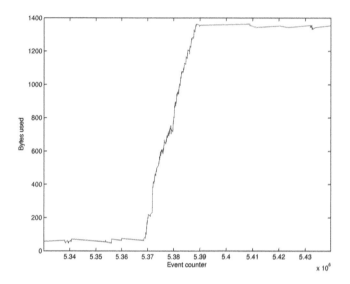

Figure 7.3: Memory usage by the list of misc lists (burst magnification)

the size of the list of misc lists. Figure 7.2 clearly shows three anomalies, where the size of the list drops almost to zero. At these points, the coalescing list was constructed, leading to the emptying and deletion of the misc lists. We said earlier that the list of misc lists emptied *almost* to zero, because the header of that list is never freed and still consumes some memory.

The first two occurrences of coalescing show that there is no correlation between coalescing and the resulting memory consumption by the list of misc lists. This is confirmed when we examine the third occurrence closely. It consists of three consecutive coalescings, as seen in the magnification in Figure 7.4, where coalescing event curve is superimposed over the sawtooth-like curve of the list of misc lists. The graph shows that only after the first coalescing in this series, there were less lists in use than before. We have, however, observed an opposite trend too, while doing test repetitions. We explain this phenomenon with the probabilistic nature of skip

77

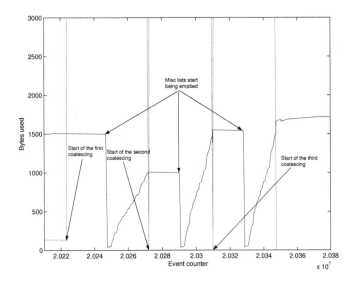

Figure 7.4: Memory usage by the list of misc lists (coalescing sequence magnification)

lists, where the level of the list – and thus the memory consumption of individual nodes – can vary from run to run[3]. This theory is supported when we, in the next section, examine the memory consumption by the extent headers and discover that the two last coalescings did not lead to any significant change in the number of extents.

Continuing to examine Figure 7.4, we observe another interesting fact. The misc lists start to get emptied and deleted from the list of misc lists approximately half-way through the coalescing process, or, in other words, almost at the very end of coalescing list construction. That means that the overwhelming majority of extents reside on quick lists and the misc lists are very sparsely populated.

Observe, that while the coalescings seem to come back-to-back,

---

[3]Random number generator is re-initialised with the system time value on initialisation of each skip list.

there must have been at list one call to *qf_free()* between them, otherwise the coalescing algorithm would not have been invoked (see Chapter 4.3.4).

After the last coalescing, the load on the list of misc lists continues to steadily grow, until it sharply reaches its maximum at the end of the simulation. We never explicitly free memory consumed by the lists and extents at the end of the simulation. The graph in Figure 7.2 ends therefore at its peak, when all extents were freed, and a considerable number of those had to be placed in a wide variety of misc list ranges. Had we freed the memory at the end of simulation, we would have observed a steadily descending ramp, reaching zero value in the end.

Extent Headers

Extent header have the highest memory consumption, claiming as much as 830KB of memory, as can be seen from the upper graph of Figure 7.5. In that figure we combine the memory load for extents in the upper curve with the memory load on the coalescing list in the lower curve to illustrate the impact of coalescing on the number of extents. The figure shows the memory consumed by *all* extents – both those residing on the free lists and those allocated and sent to the File Link Layer.

During the first part of the simulation, the number of splittings is dominating, leading to a rapid increase in extent header memory consumption. Some of the increase shows burst properties, especially the one after event number $1.1 \cdot 10^7$. We can suppose that those parts of the trace were dominated by allocation and had few or no file deletions, leading to consumption of all available extents and a constant need to create new ones.

The coalescing had a strong effect on the number of extent, when it was performed for the first time, leading to a 19% drop in memory consumption. The subsequent coalescings did not have the same effect. If we examine the magnification of the three consecutive coalescings in the lower graph of Figure 7.5, we can see that the subsequent two coalescings seemingly did not have any effect whatsoever. In fact, when we inserted additional probes and re-run the trace, we discovered that those two coalescings managed to find only two pairs of adjacent extents each. The reduction in memory

79

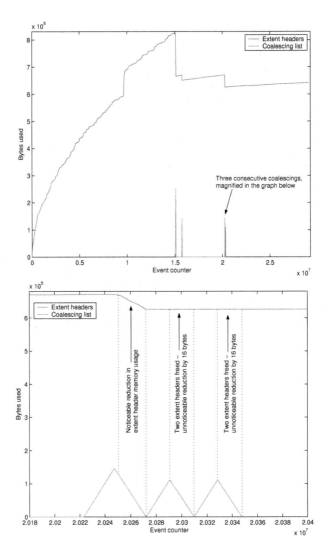

Figure 7.5: Memory usage by the extent headers in combination with coalescing

80

consumption was so negligible – only 16 bytes in each case – that it is not visible on the graphs.

These observations have two important consequences:

1. With a large enough distance between coalescings, they have a significant positive effect on the memory consumption. Coalescings should therefore be performed on a regular basis.

2. When the distance between coalescings is too small, coalescings do not have any positive effect on the memory consumption, and can even in some cases worsen it, if the reconstructed free skip lists assume a higher level. It also introduces an unnecessary computational overhead.

Further evaluation of the coalescing algorithm can be found in Section 7.2.6.

Memory Consumption by the Free Lists

Finally, we present the memory used by the free lists. It is done in conjunction with the other memory consumption to set it into proportion. We shall first look at the graph in Figure 7.6, where memory usage both the list of misc lists and the misc lists themselves are shown. The upper curve represents the misc lists. As the two curves have an order of magnitude difference in memory consumption, we use logarithmic scale on the Y-axis to allow for comparisons of the two curves. Note that both curves almost mirror each other's in their progression, which strongly suggests that there is seldom more than a couple of extents on each misc list at any given time.

We now go on to Figure 7.16, which is comprised of two graphs, showing the first and the second part of trace execution. We split the diagram into two parts partly to bring out the details and partly because the program used to generate the graphs could not handle the complete data set in one go. From top to bottom, the upper red curve is the memory consumed by the extent headers, the next, black, curve is the memory consumption of the quick lists. Lower still, the magenta curve represent the memory requirement for the misc lists, while the blue curve going along the X-axis represents

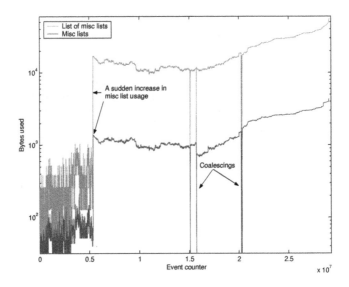

Figure 7.6: Memory usage by misc lists and their container (log. scale)

the list of misc lists. The spiky green curve is our familiar footprint of the coalescing procedure.

First, we analyse the upper graph. Memory consumption of all the components grows, though at different rates. Quick lists are the most used, while the misc lists do not become loaded in any significant way until after event $0.5 \cdot 10^7$, which is clearly visible in Figure 7.6. This can be explained with a supposition that several large files from the Helix server become freed at that moment.

The sudden burst in the number of extents is not immediately reflected in the load on the quick lists, meaning that we were right in our previous assumption that most of the newly-created extents were claimed a very short time after their creation.

In the second part of the trace execution, we again pay close attention to the effects of coalescing. Observe that coalescing first happened after more than approximately half-way through the ex-

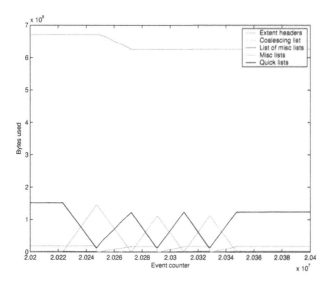

Figure 7.7: Memory usage by all components in the large partition class (magnification)

ecution. The first three coalescings had a large positive impact on the free list memory consumption, especially for the quick lists, visibly reducing their memory demand. The effect is actually proportional to the one experienced by the extent headers, which again shows that the majority of the extents resided on quick lists. In Figure 7.7 we again give a magnification of the coalescing sequence, now taking into view the effect on the free lists.

Finally, towards the end of the simulation, more files become freed than created. This gives a steady increase of the load on both free list types, while the number of extents remains fairly constant. It is interesting to examine the very end of the lower graph of Figure 7.16. There we indirectly can see the final distribution of extent sizes as quick lists occupy an order of magnitude more space than the misc lists.

83

Total Memory Consumption

	Huge	**Large**	**Medium**	**Minimum**
Misc lists	56776	55412	54280	53548
Quick lists	654260	491608	452016	476760
List of misc lists	4412	4336	4076	4340
Coalescing list	0	252152	129160	130164
Extent headers	888832	825056	649184	650784
Total	1604280	1193040	1123088	1149928

Table 7.1: Maximum memory consumption

The peak load on each allocator element in each of the partition size classes is summarised in Table 7.1. It can be summed up by a single phrase: "Bigger is not necessarily better", at least when it comes to the memory consumption by our allocator. The huge partition size, contrary to our expectations, produced the greatest memory load. After we examined the effects of coalescing on the extent header and quick list memory consumption, the reason for this behaviour becomes clear. In this class, the coalescings are never performed, which is witnessed by the zero-memory load of the coalescing list. In this case the number of extents increases unchecked, leading to a significantly larger memory load on all the parts of the allocator. This assumption is supported by Figure 7.15. There is not much difference in the memory consumption between the huge and large partition classes during the first part of the trace execution. They start to deviate from each other after the first coalescing. By the end of the execution, extent headers occupy about 900KB memory. Given that each extent header uses 16 bytes of memory, the allocator has to keep track of about 56000 extents.

Medium partition size has the best overall memory consumption footprint, most probably thanks to the relatively frequent coalescings (see Figure 7.17).

We can deem this allocator design memory-efficient, when looking at the total number of bytes required to hold the internal data structures during the execution of a relatively large trace. Even in the worst case, the allocator does not consume more than 1.6MB of main memory. This summary does not take into account the memory consumed by the return lists and the trace driver as they logically belong to the higher – File Link – layer.

For comparison purposes we present the total main memory consumption graphs for all partition size classes in Figures 7.15, 7.16, 7.17 and 7.18.

7.2.2 Computational Overhead

Partition size	User time
Huge	9m32.326s
Large	9m13.983s
Medium	9m54.562s
Minimum	10m11.061s

Table 7.2: Computational overhead

We measure the approximate value for the computational overhead by using UNIX `time` command and evaluating the time spent by the simulator in `user` mode. The test is done once for each partition size class, with AWP set to zero. All statistics collection modules are disabled, so that their overhead does not affect the timing.

Since the simulation driver has a constant overhead, the variation in execution times results from the time spent in the allocator itself[4].

As we can see from Table 7.2, the computational overhead generally increases with the decrease in the size of the free space pool, because the allocator has a progressively more complex task of finding a suitable extent. The observed increase in execution time for the huge partition class can be explained by the absence of coalescing. As we will see in Section 7.2.1, after the coalescings the allocator has fewer extents to search through, thus reducing the computational overhead.

Taking into account that the allocator has to dispatch over 14.3 million trace events, the displayed performance is very good even in the worst case scenario. When the time used by the simulation

---

[4]By deactivating the allocator, we measures that the simulation driver uses an average of 1m20.436s to read and process trace events.

85

driver is deducted from the running time of the minimum partition size class simulation, the allocator manages to perform approximately 54100 requests per second.

7.2.3 Write Operations Count and the Initial Free Space

Even the best memory footprint would not help an allocator to do its job efficiently, if it has to perform an excessive number of disk accesses to maintain the allocation state. Our allocator was carefully designed to minimise the required number of write operations.

	Number of write operations	Increase, relative to huge partition class	Operations per file
Huge	28762752	—	2.00387
Large	28768461	5709	2.00467
Medium	28768861	6109	2.00429
Minimum	28781595	18843	2.00518

Table 7.3: Write operation count for four partition sizes

Table 7.3 shows the number of write operations that the allocator had to perform, depending on the partition size class. At this stage, the AWP was set to zero, resulting in the maximum utilisation of free space.

The number of write operations can seem immensely large until we take into account the fact that there is a total of 14353600 unique files in the trace. In the third column of Table 7.3, we see how many write operations on average were required to allocates extents to each file. Even in the worst case, only marginally more than 2 write operations are required to manage a file. Considering that *one* operation is needed to allocate one extent and *one* operation is needed to free an extent, that leaves us with an average of 0.00518 operations per file spent on splitting, coalescing and multi-extent allocation in the worst case scenario.

The variation between the partition classes is not very pronounced, but the trend is clear – the less space there is, the more write operations are required. There are two factors that play in. Firstly,

86

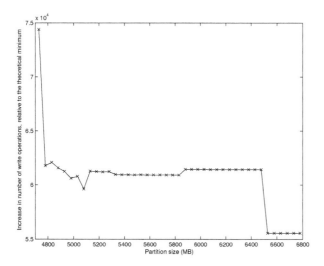

Figure 7.8: Write operation count at different partition sizes

we have an increase in coalescing activity, which results in an additional write operation for every updated extent. Secondly, with less space, the allocator is more likely to use a larger number of small extents in multi-extent allocation, resulting in more frequent splittings.

To verify this trend we performed 42 test runs[5], where partition size was incremented from the minimum until 6779MB in 50MB steps. The result of these runs is shown in Figure 7.8. The Y-axis shows the increase in the number of write operations, relative to the theoretical minimal case of two write operations per file.

The middle section of the figure shows that the number of write operations keeps at a somewhat steady level, increasing and decreasing seemingly at random, most probably depending on the order in which extents get allocated. The anomalies come in the beginning and the end of the graph. In the first run, the allocator had so little space to manage, that it was forced to perform exceedingly frequent

---

[5]The number was chosen using a certain well-defined answer.

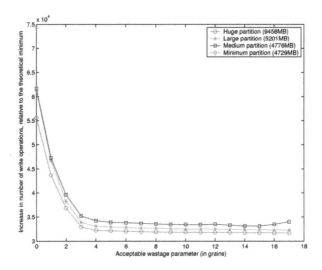

Figure 7.9: Number of write operations at different AWP settings

splittings and coalescings. Note here, how much difference 50MB of additional free space had in the near exhaustion case. For partition sizes above 6500MB, all requests could be satisfied by a single extent, thus totally avoiding coalescings and further decreasing the number of write operations to the minimum.

In this section we have seen that the allocator performs remarkably well even in a high-stress scenario.

7.2.4 Acceptable Wastage Parameter

Setting AWP to any positive non-zero value affects the effective partition size, potentially reducing the amount of space available for allocation in the process of said allocation.

We have run a test, where AWP was increased from zero to 17 grains in one grain steps. The test was repeated for all partition classes and the results are presented in Figure 7.9. Here we again used the increase in the number of write operations relative to the theoretical minimal case of two operations per file as the measure along th Y-axis.

Because AWP reduces the available space and the minimum partition class was already operating at the limit, not surprisingly, the allocator failed to provide space for that class already at AWP set to one. With sufficiently large AWP value, any initial partition size would prove to be too small and lead to a failure. In fact, the medium partition class failed at AWP equalling 18.

This leads us to the first interesting observation. The number of disk write operations was fairly constant after AWP size of 4. It went, however, slightly up for the medium class during the two test runs preceding the failure, while remaining constant for the other two classes. This is comparable with the behaviour of the minimum class at AWP zero, where the number of write operations was significantly larger than for the other classes.

AWP was in the first place introduced to reduce the number of disk accesses. It manages to do just so, as we can see from the first four test runs. At AWP of 4 grains the number of extra writes operations is almost halved. After AWP of 4 grains there is, however, no added benefit in increasing that value. As we saw from the case of the medium partition class, excessively large AWP can even lead to increased disk activity and to a subsequent allocation failure.

Based on these observations, we can suggest that AWP of 4 gives an optimal disk access performance for the allocator an it should not exceed this value.

7.2.5 Fragmentation

One of the key goals of the design of our allocator, was to keep all types of fragmentation at the lowest possible value. In this chapter we will see how the allocator manages this task.

File fragmentation

As we mentioned earlier, file fragmentation arises whenever the contents of a file has to be split over several extents. We call the additionally required extents as *excess* extents. File fragmentation can be measured in two ways:

1. we can measure it as an average number of extents per file, or

2. alternatively, we can measure the percentage of *split files*, relative to the total number of files in the system.

These two ways of measurement yield different results. Consider a system with 100 files and 150 allocated extents, where only one file is split over 51 extents. By our definition, there are 50 excess extents in the system. If we use the first way of measurement, we can conclude that file fragmentation level is 1.5 extent per file[6]. The second way of measurement tells us, however, that fragmentation level is only 1%.

We choose the first way of measurement as we perceive it to be more accurate, when it comes to reflecting the overall performance degradation incurred by file fragmentation. This method also coincides with external fragmentation measurement method used in [IJC03]. As file fragmentation is just another aspect of external fragmentation, this makes our measurements comparable.

	Excess extents	Average	Worst
Huge	0	1.00000000	1.00000000
Large	34	1.00000237	1.00000341
Medium	105	1.00000732	1.00001053
Minimum	6454	1.00044964	1.00082787

Table 7.4: File fragmentation depending on the size of the partition

In Table 7.4 we show the file fragmentation values, along with the number of excess extents for each partition class at AWP 0. The total number of files in the simulation trace is 14353600. When fragmentation level is 1, each file is placed in exactly one extent, as seen in the case of the huge partition class. For the minimum partition class, we see that the worst fragmentation level is almost twice as high as the average case, most probably occurring when the majority of the large files from the Helix server had to be allocated.

When we look at the general case, we see that at fragmentation ratio of 1.00082787 extents per file in the worst case, the level of file fragmentation is exceptionally low for all classes.

---

[6]Which is equivalent to 50%.

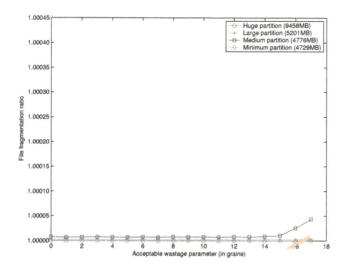

Figure 7.10: File fragmentation at different AWP settings

File fragmentation for all partition classes and AWP settings is presented in Figure 7.10. The first impression we get while examining the figure, is that the level of file fragmentation is not very dependent on the AWP setting and the size of the partition. In fact, it is only when the free space starts reaching a critically low level, that we experience the highest level of file fragmentation.

Note the lonely marker for the minimum partition size class at AWP 0. It is located in the upper left corner of the graph at a remarkable distance from the prevailing trend. We can also see the same situation when the medium partition size starts experiencing more file fragmentation as it comes closer to the point of free space exhaustion, starting at AWP 15.

Otherwise, the file fragmentation holds itself at a constant level, showing that the allocator is for the most part capable of satisfying requests with just one extent.

Internal fragmentation at Peak Load

	Extra bytes used	Internal fragmentation
Huge	7979580	1.00161197
Large	7979580	1.00161197
Medium	7980092	1.00161207
Minimum	8030780	1.00162231

Table 7.5: Average internal fragmentation at peak load depending on the size of the partition

The value for internal fragmentation is calculated, dividing the number of allocated bytes by the number of bytes requested at peak allocation. Note that this also includes the disk space used for the extent headers. The measurements are performed for all partition size classes with AWP varying from 0 to 17. As it was mentioned in the previous section, tests with $AWP > 0$ fail to complete for the minimum partition class.

Table 7.5 shows the number of additional bytes used to satisfy a peak sum of requests for 4950202308 bytes for each partition size class at AWP set to zero grains. The fragmentation is almost equal for all partition classes, but is slightly more pronounced for the minimum class, which is directly tied to the experienced higher level of file fragmentation. This is due to the fact that in our measurement of internal fragmentation, we also include space used for the on-disk extent headers. As file fragmentation increases, so does the need to store additional header information. Without this factor, the internal fragmentation levels for all partition classes would have been equal.

Interestingly, the actual minimum internal fragmentation is not much larger than our estimation done during the trace analysis in Appendix B.2.3

What influences the internal fragmentation the most is the extra storage allocated due to increase in the value of the Acceptable Wastage Parameter. This dependency is shown in Figure 7.11.

We can see that the internal fragmentation level increases almost linearly with the increase in AWP. The slope becomes slightly steeper after AWP passes 4 grains. At 15 grains of AWP, the internal frag-

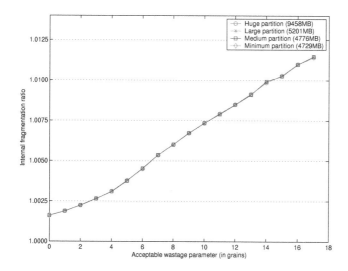

Figure 7.11: Internal fragmentation at different AWP settings

mentation passes the 1.0100 marker[7], meaning that more than 50MB of storage becomes wasted. This is, by far, not acceptable. As we saw from the write count analysis of Figure 7.9, there is little to gain from setting AWP to a larger value than 4 grains, and the improvement in write access performance experienced from increasing AWP from 3 to 4 grains is relatively limited. Coupled with the knowledge of the linear increase ratio in internal fragmentation, these experiments suggest that the value of three grains in the Acceptable Wastage Parameter is, indeed, acceptable and gives an optimal balance between wasted space and gained write throughput.

Internal Fragmentation Throughout the Trace Execution

In the previous section we looked at the fragmentation level at peak allocation. This type of measurement give the best average statis-

---

[7]Equals to 1% internal fragmentation.

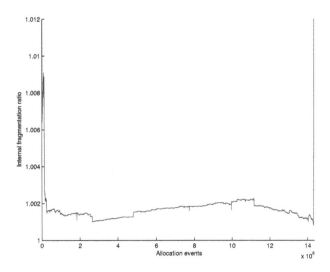

Figure 7.12: Internal fragmentation level throughout the trace execution

tics, but hides possible anomalies.

We have therefore run an additional simulation with large partition size class and AWP set to zero grains and measured the level of internal fragmentation after each allocation. The results are presented in Figure 7.12. To enhance the readability of the long-term fragmentation levels, the Y-axis of the graph was limited to displaying the internal fragmentation ratio of up to 1.012.

We can conclude from the graph that the level of internal fragmentation was fairly stable, oscillating around our previously-measured peak load fragmentation. The anomalies occur in the beginning and in the end of the simulation, where only a handful of files are managed. In those cases the fragmentation level can become heavily skewed if the majority of files are below one grain in size.

As the number of files grows, so does the statistical base, leading to the more representative measurement in the middle section of the graph.

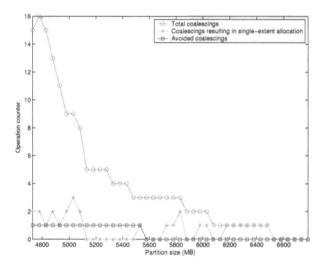

Figure 7.13: Coalescing performance at different partition sizes

7.2.6 Coalescing Measurements

We have already seen some of the effect coalescing has in the chapter covering memory load measurement. Here, we will give more data on coalescing performance and its impact on the system.

Operation Counts

As we saw from Figure 7.8, the number of write operations dropped strongly after the partition size reached approximately 6500MB. We theorised that it was caused by the absence of coalescings after that particular partition size. Here we use the same data as the ones collected for the write test to show how coalescing performed in the same conditions.

The situation is shown in Figure 7.13. The upper curve shows the total number of coalescings that had to be performed throughout the whole simulation at each partition size. Our assumption that the number of coalescings is reduced with partition size increase is affirmed. As expected, we see that after the partition size reached 6500MB, no coalescings had to be performed at all.

Our initial measure of coalescing efficiency, was the number of multi-extent allocations that could be avoided after the coalescing. As we see from the middle curve, the coalescing had the best effect for partition sizes above 6150MB, where each coalescing resulted in a subsequent single-extent allocation. In general, we never had more than three successful coalescings in any single test, even in those cases when coalescing operations were numerous. Having said that, there was never a single case where coalescing function would not have found at least one extent to merge.

This leads us to believe that the more free space there is, the higher the probability that a coalescing would achieve the desired goal. Based on this observation, we will propose for the future work to add high- and low coalescing count watermarks to avoid too frequent coalescings (see Section 8.2).

Our rudimentary coalescing avoidance system – the *coalesced* flag (see Chapter 4.3.3 for details) – had any effect only $\frac{1}{3}$ of the times. Each of those times it prevented only a single coalescing, as seen from the lower curve in Figure 7.13.

Disabling Coalescing in the Near Exhaustion Scenario

We re-run the simulation with partition size class set to minimum and AWP set to zero grains, but this time disabling the coalescing function. Our aim with this test is to see how much influence the coalescing had on the resource utilisation and allocation efficiency.

The results of this test are summarised in Table 7.6. By disabling the coalescing function we avoid 15 coalescings and do not use any memory for the coalescing lists. On the other hand all other parts of allocator have experienced an increase in load. Additionally, the simulation itself took about 25% longer time to run without coalescing, strongly suggesting that the computational overhead used by the coalescing function pays off in the longer run.

Both internal fragmentation and the number of write operations increased as the files, which could be allocated one extent, now had to have several extents associated with them.

	Coalescing On	Coalescing Off	Increase
Peak internal fragmentation	1.00162231	1.00164621	1.47%
File fragmentation (avg.)	1.00044964	1.00148262	229.73%
Number of write operations	28781595	28805418	0.08%
Total memory consumption	1142884	1639544	43.89%
List of misc lists	4100	5612	36.87%
Quick lists	471328	684924	45.32%
Misc lists	52176	58512	12.14%
Extent headers	650784	890496	36.83%
Coalescing list	129448	0	-100.00%

Table 7.6: Effects of disabling the coalescing in the near exhaustion scenario

The same applies for file fragmentation level, which increased by a whole 229.73%. This clearly illustrates that even a small number of coalescings are extremely beneficial.

As the number of extents grows, so does the memory space requirement for extent headers and the load on the free lists. In this case both extent headers and quick lists accounted for the major part of the 45.32% increase in memory consumption. This trend is similar to the one observed in our tests performed with the huge partition class, where no coalescings were required.

We can conclude that far from improving system performance, the disabling of the coalescing functions places a higher toll on all allocator components.

7.2.7 Free Space Management Dynamics

To see how the pool of free disk space is managed throughout the whole simulation, we took measurements of the number of free grains each time an extent was either taken from the pool or returned to it. This test was run with large partition class and AWP

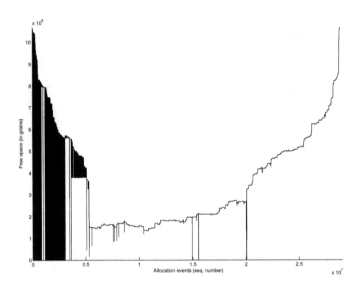

Figure 7.14: Management of the pool of free disk space

set to 0 grains. The free space management dynamics is illustrated in Figure 7.14.

These measurements include both removal of extents for the purpose of coalescing and before splitting. Thus, both operations are reflected in the graph.

The beginning of the simulation is dominated by a large amount of splittings, where an entire large extent is removed from the pool, split, and then a slightly smaller remainder extent is returned to the pool. This is the illustration of allocation from wilderness. We see this as a filled black area on the graph. This area is in fact a rapid alternation between zero and maximum number of free grains.

A similar phenomenon occurred just before event $0.5 \cdot 10^7$, where a series of allocations were performed by splitting a large extent into progressively smaller extents, without actually touching the largest extent(s) in the pool. The filled area does therefore not go below

98

$4 \cdot 10^6$ grains. The algorithm proposed by Iyengar et al in [IJC03] would have used wilderness allocation also in this case.

After that, several large files were allocated, resulting in a large drop in the amount of free space.

From there on, the allocation went largely without splittings, satisfying the requests from the free lists. We say that the allocator reached a steady state.

At event $1.5 \cdot 10^7$ the coalescings started to be performed, emptying the pool and then returning it to the previous state as far as the number of free grains is concerned.

After event $2 \cdot 10^7$ the allocator enters the final phase of the simulation, where space freeing is dominating.

7.3 Summary

We have performed a score of evaluation measurements of our allocator's performance. Some tests can be compared to the ones performed for PMFLF, while other are unique to our system.

The comparable results cover the measurement of the fragmentation levels. Our system outperforms PMFLF in this field. The best measure internal fragmentation of PMFLF is 1.03000 [IJC03, Table 6], while the *worst* level of internal fragmentation in our allocator was 1.00162, which means that our allocator performed 185 times better than PMFLF. This is especially interesting when we take into account the file size distribution that our allocator and PMFLF had wot work with. The file size distribution presented for PMFLF [IJC03, Figure 25] had the majority of files, which are smaller than 20000 bytes, whereas our file size distribution had a wider range of predominant sizes, reaching as high as 100000 bytes (see Appendix B.2.2). This means that our allocator had to make harder placement decisions than PMFLF.

File fragmentation cannot be compared directly as PMFLF does not support fragmenting of files. If we, on the other hand, recall that file fragmentation is another aspect of external fragmentation, we can cautiously compare these values. We can see from [IJC03, Figure 14] and [IJC03, Figure 17] that external fragmentation in PMFLF starts at approximately 1.05 and increases with variation of the allocator parameters, going as high as 2.0 for with a sufficiently large number of replacements. Our allocator keeps file fragmentation below 1.00005 and only comes as high as 1.00045 when the storage space is close to exhaustion. As our system supports file fragmentation, it can utilise storage space much more efficiently. At the same time, the low level of file fragmentation indicates that this feature is used sparingly.

Our other measurements do not have counterparts in PMFLF. We therefore leave it to future work to perform in-depth comparison studies of the two systems. Our results, however, indicate that the new allocator performs well in all aspects and can be integrated with some existing file system or used in design of a whole new file system for application, which place strict demands on space utilisation, speed and memory efficiency.

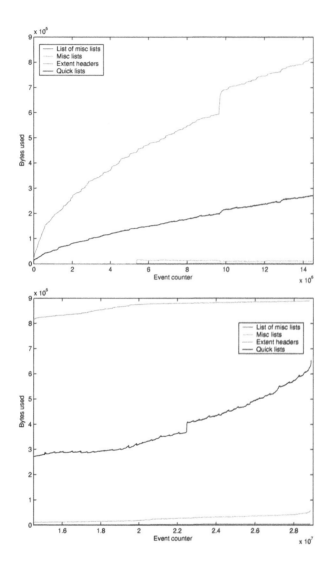

Figure 7.15: Memory usage of the huge partition class

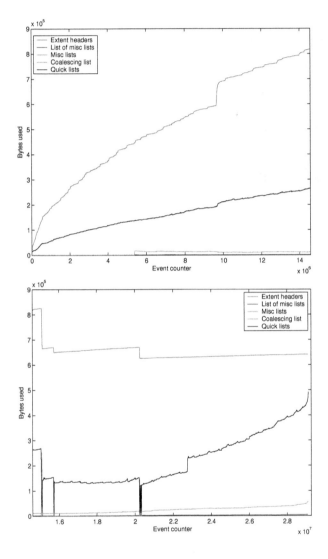

Figure 7.16: Memory usage of the large partition class

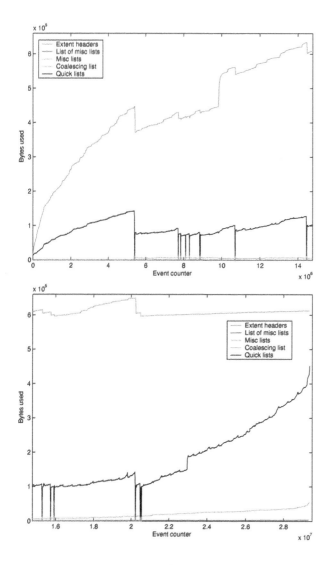

Figure 7.17: Memory usage of the medium partition class

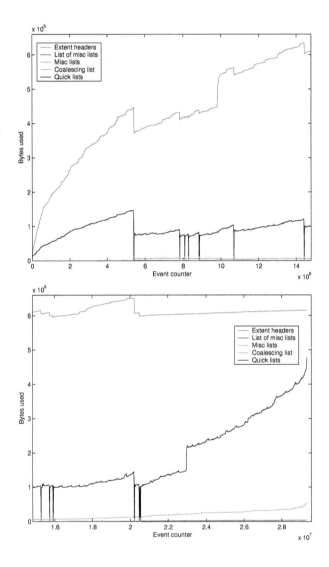

Figure 7.18: Memory usage of the minimum partition class

Chapter 8

Conclusions

8.1 Summary of Contributions

This thesis has two major contributions:

- modifications of the allocator design proposed in [IJC03], and

- extensive evaluation of the allocator's performance.

We have proposed, implemented and tested an allocator design, which uses QuickFit allocation scheme and is based on extents. This design allows us to manage free space in an efficient manner. This goal is achieved by allowing the allocator to maintain a list of contiguous segments of free space instead of disjoint blocks of equal size.

QuickFit was originally designed to internally use simple data structures, such as a singly-linked list. Our use of skip lists opens for a more efficient organisation of data and a faster implementation of the allocator's sub-algorithms.

By not keeping track of wilderness as a separate entity, but treating it as any other free extent and not distinguishing between small and large allocation requests, we have simplified the allocator implementation with no adverse effects.

Our second major contribution lies in the extensive tests performed to evaluate all aspects of the allocator's performance. We have evaluated not only how the allocator manages free disk space, but also its own impact on the overall system performance, by measuring its memory consumption and the required disk operation overhead needed to manage the free space pool. The evaluations were performed using an allocation trace, extracted from the real file access events and file size distribution.

The evaluations showed that the allocator performs well in all tests. It has a very small memory footprint, even when the number of operations is very large. The allocator keeps both internal- and file fragmentation at very low values. In many cases the fragmentation is more than 100 time lower than in comparable systems. It manages to achieve this without an excessive number of disk operations, maintaining the average number close to the minimum of two disk operations per file. The allocator also has a low computational overhead, even when the pool of free space is close to exhaustion.

In conclusion, we have designed and implemented and allocator, which in out tests outperforms comparable systems. At 2000 lines of C code, it is easy to implement and maintain. Its modular design allows for an easy incorporation into existing file systems for use in CDN proxy caches.

8.2 Future Work

In this thesis we worked with many aspects of our extent-based allocator. However, there are many possibilities for further improvement and fine tuning of the allocator. Some of the work that can be done to improve performance is also beyond the scope of this thesis because it touches on the areas used by other layers of a file system. Below, we present an overview of what further work can be done with the allocator and the surrounding system.

It would be interesting to compare the efficiency of our algorithm to the one presented in [IJC03] with regard to placement decisions and their impact on fragmentation. As this system is designed in a layered fashion, it would be easy to replace the optimised allocator with PMFLF. The same sets of allocation requests can then be run through both implementations and resulting allocation decisions compared.

106

The allocator is not aware of the data being written to the extents which it returns. It is not even aware if the extents from two different allocations might be used to store data from the same file. Such knowledge is, however, important should the space requests from growing files be managed optimally. For this purpose our allocator implements the continuity and locality hints. Because of the properties of the traces that we have at our disposal, we never make use of those hints. We feel, however, that investigating the effects of hints provided from the File Link layer on the allocation decisions can be a topic of a separate study.

The trace used in our study required a little over 4,6GB of space to be managed by the allocator. This also imposed a natural limit on the maximum number of extents present on free lists at any given time. As the result, the maximum memory footprint of the allocator was also limited and never exceeded manageable bounds. On partitions with several terabytes of data consisting of both small and large files, the memory requirement could become unmanageable. In such environment it would be reasonable to purge parts of the free lists to disk, if they become too long. This has several implications:

- not all extents will be available for analysis, so the allocation requests would return sub-optimal results;

- the coalescing would run sub-optimally as fetching extent headers from disk for the purpose of coalescing can be prohibitively expensive;

- the allocator would have to use additional disk space for its own needs. The requirements on the bookkeeping disk space cannot be determined at the time of partition creation and must be satisfied on the fly.

This scenario presents enough materials for a study in its own right.

Currently, the simulation is run in one continuous session. In real life, a file system needs to be mounted an unmounted as a system is brought to a halt or restarted. This can be simulated by fully implementing functions *qf_start()* and *qf_stop()* and stopping the simulation at several arbitrary points. The state of the allocator then has to be written to disk, using the allocator itself to provide the space for the state information. Providing space for internal structures will alter the state of the allocator and affect the next allocation after resume point, creating a cascade effect.

The logarithmic search and insertion times of skip lists open for a possibility to replace several misc lists with a single misc list as it was presented in Weinstock's [Wei76] work. Splitting of a misc list into a set of ranged misc lists was in the first place introduced by Iyengar [Iye96] as a crude form of a skip list, allowing the allocator to find the needed subset in a fast manner. This suggestion is backed by our observation in Section 7.2.1, that individual misc lists seldom hold more than a few extents each. As both the list of misc lists and the misc lists themselves are organised in skip lists, merging them will still retain the logarithmic operation times, while substantially reducing the complexity of the allocator implementation. We leave it to future work to investigate if this assumption holds.

The next suggestion for future work development, comes with regard to the coalescing algorithm. Based on the evaluation of its consequences on performance and resource utilisation, we can propose a change in our design for the activation of the coalescing algorithm. Recall that currently, the algorithm is only activated if at least one extent freeing occurred since the last coalescing. We propose adding a high and low watermarks for the number of freeing operations. Avoiding coalescing if the low watermark is not reached and forcing a coalescing if the freeing counter exceeds the high watermark. An eventual work, based on this suggestion must find the suitable values for the watermarks and investigate the impact on the whole system by this change in design.

Bibliography

[Bec82]   Leland L. Beck. A dynamic storage allocation technique based on memory residence time. *Communications of the ACM*, 25(10):714–724, October 1982.

[Dav99]   Brian D. Davison. A survey of proxy cache evaluation techniques. In *Proceedings of the Fourth International Web Caching Workshop (WCW99)*, pages 67–77, San Diego, CA, March 1999.

[IJC02]   Arun K. Iyengar, Shudong Jin, and Jim Challenger. Efficient algorithms for persistent storage allocation, 2002.

[IJC03]   Arun K. Iyengar, Shudong Jin, and Jim Challenger. Techniques for efficiently allocating persistent storage. *Journal of Systems and Software*, 68(2):85–102, 2003.

[Iye96]   Arun Iyengar. Scalability of dynamic storage allocation algorithms. In *Proceedings of the Sixth IEEE Symposium on the Frontiers of Massively Parallel Computation*, pages 223–232, October 1996.

[Knu73]   Donald E. Knuth. *The Art of Computer Programming*, volume 1: Fundamental Algorithms. Addison-Wesley, Reading, Massachusetts, 1973. First edition published in 1968.

[KV85]   David G. Korn and Kiem-Phong Vo. In search of a better malloc. In *Proc. USENIX Summer 1985*, pages 489–506, Portland, Oregon, June 1985. USENIX Association.

[LNE]   La Nueva España, http://www.lne.es/.

[Lun97]   Ketil Lund. Hovedoppgave i databehandling. Master's thesis, Department of Informatics, University of Oslo, 1997.

[MEC⁺]   Jim Mostek, William Earl, Russell Cattelan, Kenneth Preslan, et al. Porting the SGI XFS file system to Linux.

[Nor03]   Peter Norton. Online help reference for Norton Speed-Disc utility, 2003.

[Pug89]   William Pugh. Skip lists: A probabilistic alternative to balanced trees. In *Workshop on Algorithms and Data Structures*, pages 437–449, 1989.

[Ran69]   Brian Randell. A note on storage fragmentation and program segmentation. *Communications of the ACM*, 12(7):365–372, July 1969.

[Roa76]   John Roach. Development of a syntax to describe file systems used by various operating systems. Master's thesis, Department of Computer Science, University of Wales, Swansea, February 1976.

[SDH⁺96]   A. Sweeney, D. Doucette, W. Hu, C. Anderson, M. Nishimoto, and G. Peck. Scalability in the XFS file system. In *Proceedings of the USENIX 1996 Technical Conference*, pages 1–14, San Diego, CA, USA, 22–26 1996.

[Ste83]   C. J. Stephenson. Fast fits: New methods for dynamic storage allocation. In *Proceedings of the Ninth Symposium on Operating Systems Principles*, pages 30–32, Bretton Woods, New Hampshire, October 1983. ACM Press. Published as *Operating Systems Review 17*(5), October 1983.

[Tan01]   Andrew S. Tannenbaum. *Modern Operating Systems*, chapter 10.6, pages 732–753. Prentice-Hall, second edition, 2001.

[Wei76]   Charles B. Weinstock. *Dynamic Storage Allocation Techniques*. PhD thesis, Carnegie-Mellon University, Pittsburgh, Pennsylvania, April 1976.

[WJNB95] Paul R. Wilson, Mark S. Johnstone, Michael Neely, and David Boles. Dynamic storage allocation: A survey and critical review. Technical report, University of Texas at Austin Department of Computer Sciences, Kinross, Scotland, UK, 1995.

[WW88] Charles B. Weinstock and William A. Wulf. Quick fit: an efficient algorithm for heap storage allocation. *ACM SIGPLAN Notices*, 23(10):141–144, October 1988.

Appendix A

Glossary

Block In this paper a block is a fixed-size unit, used in the context of hard disk storage allocation. A block's size is a multiple of hard disk sector size.

Boundary tags A memory allocation mechanism used to simplify the process of locating neighbouring blocks for the purpose of coalescing.

Coalescing An allocation algorithm used to satisfy relatively large request, where no sufficiently large contiguous extent is present, by merging two or more neighbouring extents.

Code bytes An error detection facility, which is used to recover the start of wilderness after a system failure if deferred wilderness pointer updates were used.

Exact list A variation of segregated free lists, where each lists holds extents of exactly the same size.

Extent A dynamically adjustable hard disk unit, occupying one or more consecutive sectors.

Extent header Bookkeeping information stored within the first 64 bits of an extent. Typically used to store size and allocation status information.

External fragmentation occurs when no single fragment of free space is sufficient to satisfy a request even though the sum of all free space fragments exceeds the request size.

File A sequence of bytes, spread over one or more extents and associated with a set of metadata to facilitate and easy access to the data.

File fragmentation Splitting of a file over several extents. Can lead to increase in overhead fragmentation and degradation of contiguous read performance. We measure it as the difference between the number of files and the number of extents used to store those files, calculated as a percentage value of the latter.

Grain size All extent sizes are a multiple of the grain size. Grain size typically equals the smallest transaction unit size for the intended storage media, which is a sector of 512 bytes in the case of disks and 1 byte in case of memory management systems.

Growing file Files that increase their size after they are created. The majority of files fall under this category.

Internal fragmentation Occurs when a request size is smaller than extent size or not a multiple of a grain size. We measure it as a percentage of total allocated space, not use to store payload information.

LBA Linear Block Addressing is an addressing mode used by hard disks to address sectors by their number, as opposed to specifying cylinder, track and head parameters.

Megabyte of MB is a measure of information capacity, consisting of 1024 bytes.

Minimum extent size The size of the header and at least one byte of payload, rounded up to the nearest grain size.

Misc list A variation of segregated fits scheme, where each list holds extents which are within a certain size range.

Payload The application data to be stored by a file system.

Quick list See Exact list.

Relocation Technique used to reduce file fragmentation, where file's extents are moved to become physically contiguous.

Segregated free lists Free extent handling technique, where extents of specific sizes are kept within their own designated free lists. QuickFit allocation scheme uses segregated free lists.

Sparse file File that contain holes, for which no actual storage space is allocated during a write operation to a further location in file. The size of a holes is a multiple of grain size. The techniques saves space, but can potentially worsen file fragmentation, should a write operation be performed within the hole.

Splitting An allocation technique used to satisfy relatively small requests without undue wastage of space to internal fragmentation.

Storage overhead Space wasted due to bookkeeping data, such as block bitmaps and extent headers. It becomes more pronounced as the overhead to payload ratio increases.

Wilderness The as yet untouched by the allocation algorithm region of storage space. Can be also used as an abstraction to denote the largest free extent available for allocation.

Wilderness preservation heuristic The technique used to ensure that the largest contiguous extent is split only as the last resort, thus increasing the probability that large requests can be satisfied at a later point.

Appendix B

Allocation Trace

B.1 Web Log and Trace Characteristics

All evaluations of the allocator performance are based on the data collected from the logs of web and streaming servers of the *La Nueva España* newspaper [LNE]. The web logs were parsed to generate a trace of creation and deletion requests..

The trace contains a sequence of *allocate* and *delete* events. All events are associated with a file Id number. *Allocate* events have in addition the information about the file size and two bit flags. The first flag indicates whether a particular file entry is later replaced with a new one of another size. The other bit flag says if a file entry's deletion time was adjusted. These bits are used by our analysis tools and are not parsed by the allocator. The trace does not give any indication as to what and how often something is being written to or read from those files.

A file's creation time is determined by the first occurrence of a URL in the logs. As the web logs do not contain explicit deletion times, we have to estimate those, based on the access information, available from the logs. Deletion times are set as follows:

1. if the same instance of a file is referenced more than once, the last reference is treated as a file's deletion time;

2. if a file instance is replaced by a new one, the file's deletion event is recorded prior to replacement;

117

3. if a file is never referenced again before the end of the log, its deletion time is set to 2/3 of the distance between the last event and the creation event. It is in this case that we set the deletion adjustment bit flag.

We can alternatively set the deletion instance of the last case to the end of the trace, in which case all files that are not replaced will be kept until the end of simulation. We leave it to future work to investigate the consequences of such choice.

The two web logs that we parse and merge represent the files fetched from an HTTP server and from a Helix server. Files from the HTTP server are HTML text files and miscellaneous images, which size seldom exceeds one megabyte. Helix files, on the other hand, are comparatively large, often spanning tens of megabytes.

The trace is executed in one session, without any stops. We leave it to future work to analyse possible implications of trace execution suspension with the following preservation of the internal allocator state.

B.2 Trace Analysis

The allocation trace was analysed for replacement and size distributions. Here we present the key characteristics of this trace.

The initial web log contained over 138.8 million entries. Of these entries, there are only 14.35 million operations that we treat as allocations, covering 67929 unique file URLs. The remaining entries are either invalid or discarded read operations. 1.78 million allocations are of zero-length lifetime type, meaning that those allocations are immediately followed by a deallocation.

B.2.1 Replacement Distribution

As we just saw, there are many more allocations than the actual unique file names, which means that the majority of operations are replacements. By replacement we mean a situation when a file is deleted to be immediately replaced by another file with the same URL name, but a new file size.

118

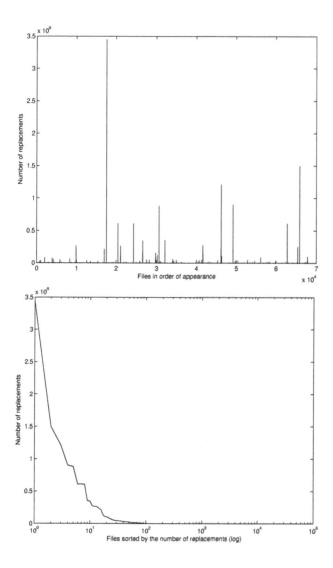

Figure B.1: File replacement distribution

In fact, there are 14.28 million replacements. When we look at the replacement distribution in the upper graph of Figure B.1, we can describe it as "spiky", meaning that a minority of files are responsible for the largest number of replacements. Only 1975 files ever get replaced, while 10 of those files are responsible for the overwhelming majority of replacements, which is clearly seen in the lower logarithmic graph of Figure B.1.

The maximum space used to accommodate the allocated files at any given time is 4,61GB. However, the cumulative size of all allocation requests throughout the whole simulation is 51.20GB.

B.2.2 File Size Distribution

Analysing size distribution of the traces, we distinguish between distribution of all allocation sizes and the final snapshot of allocations, using the replacement flag stored in the generated trace. We denote the first version as *with replacements* (WR) and the second version as *no replacements* (NR) respectively. WR distribution can be treated as a *cumulative* load on the allocator throughout the whole of the execution. We consider and describe the WR distribution as the most interesting for us because it covers all the requests that will go through the allocator. NR distribution is interesting in its own right as a one-time snapshot of the allocation state once there are no more pending allocation requests in the queue. We will use it to estimate the expected internal fragmentation in Section B.2.3.

Over 50% of all allocations in the trace are for files which are smaller than 576 bytes, and would thus fit within two grains, when the grain size is set to 512 bytes. Almost 4% of the files in the trace are 258 byes, making that a dominating file size. There are 46702 unique file sizes, with an average file size being 3829 bytes. The largest allocation in the trace is for 902726025 bytes or 861MB. The upper graph of Figure B.2 shows the file size distribution of all the files in the trace. The file distribution in this trace clearly approximates the probabilistic Pareto distribution presented in Figure 4.1 from Chapter 4.1. To visualise it even more, we created a magnified section of the lower file sizes, shown in the lower graph of Figure B.2. From this graph we can see that the most frequent file sizes are below 100000 bytes. After 400000 bytes we observe a re-

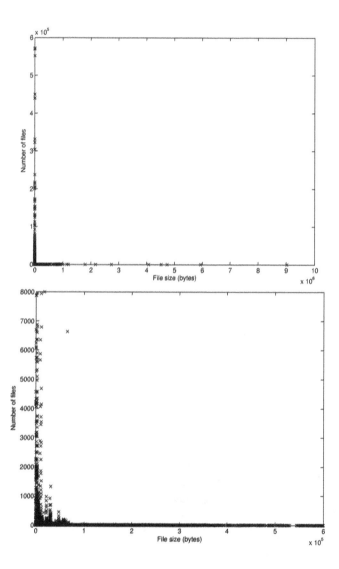

Figure B.2: File size distribution

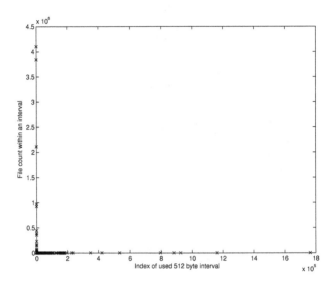

Figure B.3: File size distribution in 512 byte intervals

duction in the number of occurrences of even the single instances of some file sizes. The number of occurrences drops dramatically after approximately 100MB.

We then study the distributions grouped into 512 byte large bins, taking into account that additional 8 bytes will be spent for header information. At this stage we assume that enough space is provided to always allocate one extent for each file.

The graph in Figure B.3 shows that the grouped distribution follows the general file size distribution. The intervals after the 20000th are very sparsely populated.

The most interesting characteristics of the grouping become apparent when we magnify the graph and view the load on the first 2000 intervals, while truncating the view at 6000 occurrences. This is shown in the upper graph of Figure B.5. Both figures are derived from the WR distribution and show clearly which free lists were the most frequently used. We can therefore view this 512 byte group-

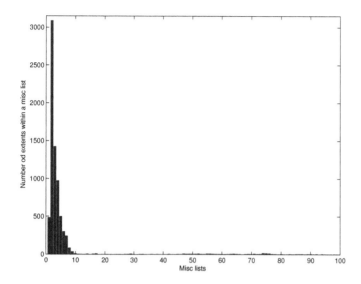

Figure B.4: The load on misc lists accommodating 200 intervals

ing as a fair representation of the expected load on the free lists in our allocator. The part of the graph displaying the most load would correspond to the quick list segment of the allocator, while the remaining part would be covered by misc lists.

Looking at the lower graph of Figure B.5, we can state that the upper boundary of quick lists should be set to 150 intervals, as those intervals will be the most populated ones. To determine the range of the individual misc lists, we have to look the expected number of extents within each misc list at that range. From the lower graph we can see that there is an average of 15 occurrences per interval after the 150th interval. This means that we can expect 3000 extents within a 200 interval group in the worst case. This is confirmed by Figure B.4, which shows the load on the first 100 misc lists. Using 200 intervals per misc list, we get a decreasing load, starting with approximately 3000 extents in the second misc list. The first misc list has a lower number of extents, because some of the extents from that range belong to the quick list segment.

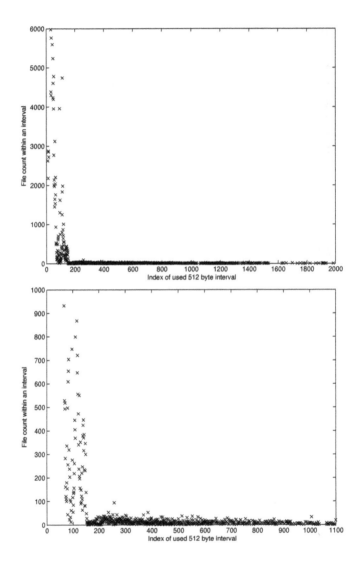

Figure B.5: File size distribution in 512 byte intervals (magnifications)

124

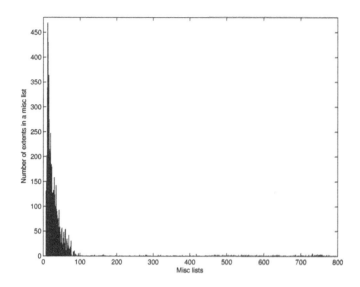

Figure B.6: The load on misc lists accommodating 20 intervals

Given that the most loaded quick lists can have up to 4 million extent stored in them in the worst case, 3000 extents does not seem like a large value.

We have, however, to take into account the algorithmic specifics of fetching an extent from a misc list (see Chapter 4.3.3). Whereas the first available extent is fetched from a quick list, misc lists are searched for the best fit, with a possible addition of the best address locality. It is therefore in the interest of allocation speed performance to keep misc lists as short as possible, balancing the number of misc lists and their length. As we cannot avoid having a large number of misc lists that contain only one or two large-sized extents, we have to concentrate on optimising the load on the misc lists containing medium-sized extents.

From Figure B.4 we can see that in our scenario of 200 intervals per misc lists, only the first 10 misc lists out of 265 non-empty ones have any significant load. Searching for the correct misc list is less expensive as searching within a misc list, so reducing the size of each misc list, while doubling the number of misc lists, until they are approximately equal would be beneficial for the extent search times. At the same time we can expect that the number of misc lists containing only one or two extents will remain fairly constant as the distance between the large-sized extents is larger than our initial range size. Given the above data, we can calculate that the optimal misc list range size would be approximately 20 intervals per misc list. This situation is shown in Figure B.6, where we display the load on the first 800 misc lists. In this scenario, the first 85 misc lists are the most loaded, containing up to 470 extents in the worst case and 99 extent on average. The total number of non-empty misc lists has increased to 614 misc lists. It represent an increase by 2.3 times, while the average load on the most used misc lists was reduced by 7.2 times. Given that searching within the misc lists requires an extra comparison, compared to the search of an appropriate misc list itself, we can expect a roughly sevenfold gain in misc list search times.

B.2.3 Expected Internal Fragmentation

We can estimate that the internal fragmentation ratio will be approximately 1.001306 bytes allocated over bytes requested. It is done by analysing the expected final state of the free lists in NR distribution, with grain size set to 512 bytes and extent header overhead set to 8 bytes.

Appendix C

Source Code

C.1 Common Code

These files are used both by the trace generator, the allocator and the file size analysis suite.

C.1.1 storage_types.h

```
 1  #ifndef STORAGE_TYPES_H
 2  #define STORAGE_TYPES_H
 3
 4  /*
 5   * An entry in a raw cleaned binary trace (input)
 6   */
 7  struct raw_trace {
 8      unsigned char    url[8];
 9      unsigned int     bytes_sent;
10      unsigned short   status;
11  } __attribute__((packed));
12
13
14  /*
15   * The entries for the the binary allocation trace. Operation code is
16   * part of the flags member. The flags for the alloc_trace struct's
17   * states member. Only used for statistical purposes. Bit 1 is set if
18   * the file entry was replaced by another size. Bit 5 is set if
19   * deleted value is adjusted
20   */
21  #define OP_CREATE     1
22  #define OP_DELETE     2
23  #define FL_REPLACED  16
24  #define FL_DELMOD    32
25
26  struct alloc_trace {
27      unsigned int     file_id;
28      unsigned int     size;     //set to 0 if operation is "delete"
29      unsigned char    flags;    //Contains OP_ and FL_ flags
30  } __attribute__((packed));
31
32  #endif
```

C.1.2 libarg.h

127

```
 1  #ifndef __LIBARG_H_
 2  #define __LIBARG_H_
 3
 4  #ifndef BOOL_T
 5  #define BOOL_T
 6  typedef enum {
 7    FALSE,
 8    TRUE,
 9  } bool_t;
10  #endif
11
12  //Prototype of the only function
13  bool_t parseArgs(int argc, char **argv,
14                   const char *name, bool_t isSwitch, char **par);
15
16  #endif
```

C.1.3   libarg.c

```
 1  /*
 2   *  Standard argument parsing routine
 3   */
 4
 5  #include <string.h>
 6
 7  #include "libarg.h"
 8
 9  /*
10   *  The function goes through the arguement list in search of argument
11   *  'name'. If the argument exists, TRUE is returned. If isSwitch flag
12   *  is not set, then the argument is parametric and the function
13   *  returns the parameter to the argument in '*par' (the next entry in
14   *  the list). If parameter does not exist TRUE is still returned, but
15   *  *par is set to NULL.
16   */
17  bool_t parseArgs(int argc, char **argv,
18                   const char *name, bool_t isSwitch, char **par){
19    register int i;
20
21    //Nullify the return parameter if it is given.
22    if(par != NULL)
23      *par = NULL;
24
25    for(i = 1; i < argc; i++){
26      if(strcmp(name, argv[i]) == 0){
27        if(!isSwitch && (argv[i+1] != NULL)){
28          *par = argv[i+1];
29        }
30        return TRUE;
31      }
32    }
33
34    return FALSE;
35  }
```

C.2 Allocator

The allocator is spread over several source files, following the layered design and the principals of modularity. Header files are used to bind the various parts of the code together. `skiplist.c` contains all the code needed for Skip list management. `simalloc.c` is the simulation driver, which reads the trace and issues the allocation and deallocation requests to the allocator. I represents a rudimentary File Link layer implementation. `allocator.c` and `alloc_helper.c` contain the main and auxiliary functions of the Allocation layer implementation. `media.c` holds the two functions of the Media I/O layer. `memory.c` and `alloc_stat.c` contain the code for collection of statistical information used in our evaluations.

C.2.1 common.h

```
1  #ifndef COMMON_H
2  #define COMMON_H
3
4  #include <stdint.h>
5
6  //#define DEBUG
7
8  #ifndef BOOL_T
9  #define BOOL_T
10 typedef enum {
11    FALSE,
12    TRUE,
13 } bool_t;
14 #endif
15
16 typedef uint64_t asize_t; // Address size in grains
17
18 /*
19  * Parameters describing an extent. Both extent and address sizes are
20  * grains (which are equal to LBA values).
21  */
22 struct extent{
23    asize_t      size;
24    asize_t      address;
25 };
26
27 void errstop(char *msg, int code);
28
29 #endif
```

C.2.2 skiplist.h

```
1  #ifndef SKIPLIST_H
2  #define SKIPLIST_H
3
4  #include "common.h"
5  #include "memory.h" //For prototype of stat_*
6
7  typedef enum {
8      SL_OK,
9      SL_MEM_EXHAUSTED,
10     SL_DUPLICATE_KEY,
11     SL_KEY_NOT_FOUND,
12     SL_PAST_LAST_NODE
```

```
13   }statusEnum_t;
14
15
16   struct skip_list{
17     struct list_node *hdr;        // list Header
18     struct list_node *nil;        // Portable impl, is set == hdr
19     struct list_node *last;       //Fast access to the last element
20     int              listLevel;   // current level of list (0  to
21                                   // MAXLEVEL-1)
22     int              maxLevel;    // Portable, dynamic adjustment
23     char             dupAllowed;  //Boolean saying if dupliactes are
24                                   //allowed
25
26     //Pointer to comparison function
27     int (*compfunc)(const void *, const void *);
28
29     int              maxListLevel; //Statistical info
30     memstat_t        mem_stat;
31     void             *info;        //Pointer to optional assosiated
32                                    //data
33   };
34
35
36   //A node in a skip list. Sorting key is the data field or a part of it.
37   struct list_node{
38     void             *data;
39     struct list_node *forward[1]; //Forward pointer(s)
40   };
41
42   /*
43    * The generic implementation of SkipList functions. One of the status
44    * values is returned. delete() and find() return the data portion of
45    * the deleted or located node. The status result is returned in 'res'
46    * field. Result must always be examined On SL_KEY_NOT_FOUND, find()
47    * returns the next entry in the list.
48    *
49    * Comparison function is expected to return an integer <, == or >
50    * than 0, depending on the comparison result of the data members of
51    * the list_node structure. As comparison is performed on the data
52    * memeber level, which can contain one or more key values, the key
53    * parameter to the delete() and find() functions is a dummy data
54    * structure, equal to the one stored in the list_node structure, and
55    * initialised with the desired search criteria.
56    */
57
58   statusEnum_t sl_initList(struct skip_list *sl,
59                       int maxLevel, memstat_t memStat, bool_t dupAllowed,
60                       int (*compfunc)(const void *, const void *));
61   bool_t sl_delList(struct skip_list *sl);
62   statusEnum_t sl_insert_node(struct skip_list *sl, void *newEntry);
63   void *sl_delete_node(struct skip_list *sl, void *key, statusEnum_t *res);
64   void *sl_find_node(struct skip_list *sl, void *key, statusEnum_t *res);
65   inline bool_t sl_isEmpty(struct skip_list *sl);
66   inline void *sl_firstElem(struct skip_list *sl);
67
68
69   /* This function breaks encapsulation, but is needed by the allocator
70    * to efficientry traverse the list of misc list
71    */
72   struct list_node *sl_find_listnode(struct skip_list *sl, void *key,
73                                      statusEnum_t *res);
74
75   #endif
```

C.2.3   skiplist.c

```
1   #include <stdlib.h>
2   #include <stdio.h>
3   #include <time.h>
4   #include <string.h>
5   #include <assert.h>
6
7   #include "skiplist.h"
8
9   /*
10   * Adapted general SkipList management functions.
11   */
12
13   static int get_level(struct skip_list *sl);
14
```

```
15  /* Insert a file entry into a given SkipList */
16  statusEnum_t sl_insert_node(struct skip_list *sl, void *newEntry){
17    int i, newLevel;
18    struct list_node **update;
19    struct list_node *x;
20
21    //Dynamically initialize update array
22    update = malloc(sizeof(struct list_node *) * (sl->maxLevel + 1));
23    if(update == NULL){
24      return SL_MEM_EXHAUSTED;
25    }
26
27    /* find where key belongs */
28    x = sl->hdr;
29    for(i = sl->listLevel; i >= 0; i--) {
30      while((x->forward[i] != sl->nil) &&
31            sl->compfunc(x->forward[i]->data, newEntry) < 0)
32        x = x->forward[i];
33      update[i] = x;
34    }
35
36    /* Checking for duplicates; ignore if allowed flag is set. */
37    if(!sl->dupAllowed){
38      x = x->forward[0];
39      if((x != sl->nil) && (sl->compfunc(x->data, newEntry) == 0)) {
40        free(update);
41        return SL_DUPLICATE_KEY;
42      }
43    }
44
45    /* Create and insert a new node in the skip list. */
46    newLevel = get_level(sl);
47
48    if(newLevel > sl->listLevel){
49      update[newLevel] = sl->nil;   //NOTE! Only works with "fixed dice"
50      sl->listLevel = newLevel;
51      if(sl->listLevel > sl->maxListLevel)
52        sl->maxListLevel = sl->listLevel;
53    }
54
55    /* make new node */
56    x = stat_malloc(sizeof(struct list_node) +
57                    newLevel * sizeof(struct list_node *), sl->mem_stat);
58    if (x == NULL){
59      free(update);
60      return SL_MEM_EXHAUSTED;
61    }
62
63    x->data = newEntry;
64
65    /* update forward links */
66    for(i = 0; i <= newLevel; i++) {
67      x->forward[i] = update[i]->forward[i];
68      update[i]->forward[i] = x;
69    }
70
71    /* If the new node is the last one, update the tail pointer */
72    if(x->forward[0] == sl->nil)
73      sl->last = x;
74
75    free(update);
76
77    return SL_OK;
78  }
79
80
81  /*
82   * Delete a node corresponding to the provided tick from the skip list
83   * and then return the associated file structure. If none found, NULL
84   * pointer is returned.
85   */
86  void *sl_delete_node(struct skip_list *sl, void *key, statusEnum_t *res){
87    int i;
88    struct list_node **update;
89    struct list_node *x;
90    void *tmp;
91
92    assert(res != NULL);
93
94    //Dynamically initialize update array
95    update = malloc(sizeof(struct list_node *) * (sl->maxLevel + 1));
96    if(update == NULL){
97      *res = SL_MEM_EXHAUSTED;
```

131

```
98       return NULL;
99    }
100
101   /* find where data belongs */
102   x = sl→hdr;
103   for (i = sl→listLevel; i >= 0; i−−) {
104     while ((x→forward[i] != sl→nil) &&
105            (sl→compfunc(x→forward[i]→data, key) < 0))
106       x = x→forward[i];
107
108     update[i] = x;
109   }
110   x = x→forward[0];
111   if ((x == sl→nil) || sl→compfunc(x→data, key) != 0){
112     free(update);
113     *res = SL_KEY_NOT_FOUND;
114     return NULL;
115   }
116
117   /* If the node to be deleted is the last one, update the tail pointer */
118   if(x→forward[0] == sl→nil)
119     sl→last = update[0];
120
121
122   /* adjust forward pointers */
123   for (i = 0; i <= sl→listLevel; i++) {
124     if (update[i]→forward[i] != x) break;
125     update[i]→forward[i] = x→forward[i];
126   }
127
128   /* salvage data before the node is deleted */
129   tmp = x→data;
130
131   stat_free(x, sl→mem_stat);
132
133   /* adjust header level */
134   while((sl→listLevel > 0)
135         && (sl→hdr→forward[sl→listLevel] == sl→nil))
136     sl→listLevel−−;
137
138   free(update);
139   *res = SL_OK;
140   return tmp;
141 }
142
143
144 void *sl_find_node(struct skip_list *sl, void *key, statusEnum_t *res){
145   int i;
146   struct list_node *x = sl→hdr;
147
148   /* find node containing data  */
149
150   assert(res != NULL);
151
152   for(i = sl→listLevel; i >= 0; i−−) {
153     while ((x→forward[i] != sl→nil)
154            && (sl→compfunc(x→forward[i]→data, key) < 0))
155       x = x→forward[i];
156   }
157
158   x = x→forward[0];
159   if(x != sl→nil){
160     if(sl→compfunc(x→data, key) == 0){
161       *res = SL_OK;
162     }else{
163       *res = SL_KEY_NOT_FOUND;
164     }
165     return x→data;
166   }
167
168   *res = SL_PAST_LAST_NODE;
169   return NULL;
170 }
171
172
173 /* Specially modified function!  Returns a *list_node*, which data
174  * entry is *greater or equal* to the provided key! Used to quickly
175  * locate the first suitable list of misc lists.
176  */
177 struct list_node *sl_find_listnode(struct skip_list *sl, void *key,
178                                     statusEnum_t *res){
179   int i;
180   struct list_node *x = sl→hdr;
```

132

```
181
182     assert(res != NULL);
183
184     /* find node containing data */
185
186     for(i = sl->listLevel; i >= 0; i--) {
187         while((x->forward[i] != sl->nil)
188               && (sl->compfunc(x->forward[i]->data, key) < 0))
189             x = x->forward[i];
190     }
191
192     x = x->forward[0];
193     if(x != sl->nil){
194         *res = SL_OK;
195         return x;
196     }
197
198     *res = SL_PAST_LAST_NODE;
199
200     return NULL;
201 }
202
203
204
205 /***************************
206  *    initialize skip list  *
207  ***************************/
208 statusEnum_t sl_initList(struct skip_list *sl,
209                          int maxLevel, memstat_t memStat, bool_t dupAllowed,
210                          int (*compfunc)(const void *, const void *)){
211     int i;
212
213     memset(sl, 0, sizeof(struct skip_list));
214
215     sl->hdr = stat_malloc(sizeof(struct list_node) +
216                           maxLevel * sizeof(struct list_node *), memStat);
217
218     if(sl->hdr == NULL){
219         return SL_MEM_EXHAUSTED;
220     }
221
222     sl->nil = sl->hdr;
223     sl->last = sl->hdr;
224     sl->mem_stat = memStat;
225     sl->maxLevel = maxLevel;
226     sl->compfunc = compfunc;
227     sl->dupAllowed = dupAllowed;
228     sl->maxListLevel = 0;
229     sl->hdr->data = NULL;
230
231     for (i = 0; i <= maxLevel; i++)
232         sl->hdr->forward[i] = sl->nil;
233
234     srand(time(NULL));
235
236     return SL_OK;
237 }
238
239
240 bool_t sl_delList(struct skip_list *sl){
241     if(!sl_isEmpty(sl))
242         return FALSE;
243
244     stat_free(sl->hdr, sl->mem_stat);
245
246     return TRUE;
247 }
248
249
250 inline bool_t sl_isEmpty(struct skip_list *sl){
251     return sl->hdr->forward[0] == sl->nil;
252 }
253
254
255 inline void *sl_firstElem(struct skip_list *sl){
256     assert(!sl_isEmpty(sl));
257     return sl->hdr->forward[0]->data;
258 }
259
260 /* Determine random level for the new skip list node. "Fix the dice"
261  * by allowing the new level to be at most one more than the current
262  * level of the list.
263  */
```

133

```
264  static int get_level(struct skip_list *sl){
265    int newLevel;
266
267    for(
268        newLevel = 0;
269        rand() < RAND_MAX/2
270          && newLevel < sl->maxLevel
271          && newLevel <= sl->listLevel;
272        newLevel++);
273
274    return newLevel;
275  }
```

C.2.4   simalloc.h

```
1  #ifndef SIMALLOC_H
2  #define SIMALLOC_H
3
4  /* Data structures used to represent allocated files: i.e. a linked
5   * list of extents assosiated with a file, as well a copy of its
6   * corresponding allocation trace entry.
7   */
8
9  #include "skiplist.h"
10
11  struct sim_file{
12    struct alloc_trace at;
13    struct skip_list *ext;
14  };
15
16  //Function prototypes
17  void errstop(char *msg, int code);
18  void trc_driver(char *file);
19  void create_file(struct skip_list *sl, struct alloc_trace *at);
20  void delete_file(struct skip_list *sl, struct alloc_trace *at);
21
22  #endif
```

C.2.5   simalloc.c

```
1   #include <stdlib.h>
2   #include <stdio.h>
3   #include <string.h>
4   #include <assert.h>
5
6   #include "../common/storage_types.h"
7   #include "../common/libarg.h"
8
9   #include "common.h"
10  #include "simalloc.h"
11  #include "alloc_exports.h"
12  #include "memory.h"
13  #include "skiplist.h"
14  #include "media.h"
15  #include "alloc_stat.h"
16
17
18  void errstop(char *msg, int code){
19    fprintf(stderr, "\n\nSimalloc_stopped_with_code_%d:\n\t%s\n", code, msg);
20    exit(code);
21  }
22
23
24  /*
25   * Comparison function for the driver skip list
26   */
27  int filecomp(const void *val1, const void *val2){
28    if(((struct sim_file *)val1)->at.file_id >
29       ((struct sim_file *)val2)->at.file_id)
30      return 1;
31
32    if(((struct sim_file *)val1)->at.file_id <
33       ((struct sim_file *)val2)->at.file_id)
34      return -1;
35
36    return 0;
37  }
```

134

```
38
39
40  int main(int argc, char **argv){
41    char *param;
42    char *file;
43    bool_t no_coal;
44    uint32_t psize = 0;
45    uint32_t awp = 0;
46
47    //Read the file name containing the trace.
48    parseArgs(argc, argv, "-f", FALSE, &file);
49
50    no_coal = parseArgs(argc, argv, "-nc", TRUE, NULL);
51
52    //Read the size of the partition (in MB)
53    if(parseArgs(argc, argv, "-p", FALSE, &param) && (param != NULL)){
54      psize = atol(param);
55    }
56
57    //Read the size of the Acceptable Wastage Parameter
58    if(parseArgs(argc, argv, "-w", FALSE, &param) && (param != NULL)){
59      awp = atol(param);
60    }
61
62    if((psize == 0) || (file == NULL)){
63      printf("Usage:_%s_-f_tracefile_-p_part_size_[-w_AWP_size]_[-nc]\n"
64             "\tThe_partition_size_is_in_megabytes_and_must_be_>_0.\n"
65             "The_-nc_parameter_stands_for_\"no_coalescing\"_and_turns\n"
66             "_off_that_feature.\n",
67             strrchr(argv[0],'/')+1);
68      exit(1);
69    }
70
71    //Initialise allocator statistics collection system
72    as_init();
73
74    //Initialise memory management statistical interface
75    stat_mem_init();
76
77    //Initialise Media I/O layer (the counters)
78    mediaInit();
79
80    //Initialise the allocator with a given partition size and AWP
81    qf_mkpart((uint64_t)psize * 1048576LL, awp, no_coal);
82
83
84    //Run the simulation
85    trc_driver(file);
86
87
88    //Print memory usage statistics
89    stat_mem_print();
90
91    return 0;
92  }
93
94
95  void create_file(struct skip_list *sl, struct alloc_trace *at){
96    struct sim_file *tmp;
97    statusEnum_t res;
98
99    tmp = stat_malloc(sizeof(struct sim_file), MEM_IGNORE);
100   if(tmp == NULL)
101     errstop("Out_of_memory_in_create_file\n", 1);
102
103   memcpy(&(tmp->at), at, sizeof(struct alloc_trace));
104
105   //This counter must come before the allocation request for the
106   //running internal fragmentation stat printout to work.
107   as_add_to_max_bytes(at->size);
108
109   tmp->ext = qf_alloc(at->size, FALSE, 0);
110
111   if(tmp->ext == NULL){
112     errstop("Allocator_is_out_of_space!", 9);
113   }
114
115   //Place the file into the file queue, sorted by file ID number.
116   res = sl_insert_node(sl, tmp);
117   if(res != SL_OK){
118     errstop("Driver:_Insertion_of_a_file_failed!", res);
119   }
120 }
```

135

```
121
122
123   void delete_file(struct skip_list *sl, struct alloc_trace *at){
124     struct sim_file *tmp;
125     struct sim_file key;
126     statusEnum_t res;
127
128     key.at.file_id = at->file_id;
129
130     //Remove the file with the give id from the list
131     tmp = sl_delete_node(sl, &key, &res);
132
133     //Free all extents occupied by the file
134     if(res == SL_OK){
135       as_sub_from_max_bytes(tmp->at.size);
136       qf_free(tmp->ext);
137       stat_free(tmp, MEM_IGNORE);
138     }else{
139       errstop("Critical_error_in_delete_file().\n", res);
140     }
141   }
142
143
144   /*
145    * The main driver allocation/deallocation loop is here
146    */
147   void trc_driver(char *file){
148     FILE *fin;
149     struct alloc_trace at;
150     struct skip_list file_list;
151     int c_total, c_single, c_avoid, c_nomerge;
152
153     c_total = c_single = c_avoid = c_nomerge = 0;
154
155     if((fin = fopen(file, "r")) == NULL){
156       errstop("Cannot_open_input_trace!\n", 2);
157     }
158
159     if(sl_initList(&file_list, 20,
160                    MEM_IGNORE, FALSE, &filecomp)){
161       errstop("Out_of_memory_in_trc_driver", 1);
162     }
163
164     for(;;){
165       //Read event from the trace until done.
166       if(fread(&at, sizeof(struct alloc_trace), 1, fin) != 1){
167         break;
168       }
169
170       //Perform the required operation
171       if(at.flags & OP_CREATE){
172         as_count_files();
173         create_file(&file_list, &at);
174       }else if(at.flags & OP_DELETE){
175         delete_file(&file_list, &at);
176       }
177     } //for(;;)
178
179     qf_cleanup();
180
181     fprintf(stderr, "Trace_request_high_watermark:_%llu_bytes\n",
182             as_get_max_bytes());
183     fprintf(stderr, "Adjusted_allocator_high_watermark:_%llu_grains\n",
184             as_get_max_grains());
185     fprintf(stderr, "Internal_fragmentation_(avg._at_peak_load):_%.8Lf\n",
186             as_get_ifrag_avg());
187
188     fprintf(stderr, "\nNumber_of_files_in_the_trace:_%llu\n",
189             as_get_file_count());
190     fprintf(stderr, "Total_number_of_extents_allocated:_%llu\n",
191             as_get_ext_count());
192     fprintf(stderr, "Number_of_multi-extent_allocations:_%llu\n",
193             as_get_multiallocs());
194     fprintf(stderr, "File_fragmentation_(avg._extents_/_file):_%.8Lf\n",
195             as_get_ffrag_avg());
196     fprintf(stderr, "File_fragmentation_(max._extents_/_file):_%.8Lf\n",
197             as_get_ffrag_max());
198     fprintf(stderr, "File_fragmentation_(by_multi-ext._file_count):_"
199             "%.8Lf_percent\n",
200             ((long double)as_get_multiallocs() * 100) /
201             (long double)as_get_file_count());
202
203     fprintf(stderr, "\nTotal_write_requests:_%llu\n", g_write_count);
```

136

```
204
205    as_get_coal_status(&c_total , &c_single , &c_avoid , &c_nomerge);
206
207    fprintf(stderr , "\nTotal_coalescings: %d\n", c_total);
208    fprintf(stderr , "Coalescings_leading_to_single_allocation: %d\n",
209                    c_single);
210    fprintf(stderr , "Coalescigs_with_no_mergings: %d\n", c_nomerge);
211    fprintf(stderr , "Avoided_coalescings: %d\n", c_avoid);
212 }
```

C.2.6   alloc_exports.h

```
 1  #ifndef ALLOC_EXPORTS_H
 2  #define ALLOC_EXPORTS_H
 3
 4
 5  /*
 6   * Function prototypes. qf_alloc returns a skiplist containing one or
 7   * more extents. This is done for simplicity. This way we do not need
 8   * to keep a 'next' pointer in the in-memory extent descriptors and we
 9   * can re-use the existing infrastructure.
10   */
11  void qf_mkpart(uint64_t part_size, unsigned int awp_size, bool_t no_coal);
12  void qf_start(void);
13  void qf_stop(void);
14  struct skip_list *qf_alloc(asize_t byte_size, bool_t cont_hint,
15                             asize_t loc_hint);
16  void qf_free(struct skip_list *ext);
17  void qf_cleanup(void);
18
19  #endif
```

C.2.7   allocator.h

```
 1  #ifndef ALLOCATOR_H
 2  #define ALLOCATOR_H
 3
 4  #include "common.h"
 5  #include "skiplist.h"
 6
 7  #define NUM_QUICK_LISTS 150 //QL array dimention
 8  #define GRAIN_SIZE 512 //In bytes
 9  #define MISC_RANGE 20   //Based on the trace characteristics, described
10                          //in thesis
11
12  //Maximum partition size in bytes
13  #define MAX_PART_SIZE (GRAIN_SIZE * sizeof(asize_t))
14  #define HEADER_SIZE (sizeof(asize_t))
15
16  /*
17   * This data structure describes the properties of a misc list and
18   * contains the skip list of extents stored within the mic list. It is
19   * stored as a list_node data member of the qf_allocator.ml skiplist.
20   */
21  struct misc_list{
22      asize_t        range_idx;
23      struct skip_list extents;
24  };
25
26
27  //Skip list levels — these are zero-based
28  #define COAL_LEVEL  32
29  #define QL_LEVEL    20
30  #define ML_LEVEL    16
31  #define MLL_LEVEL    6
32  #define RES_LEVEL    1
33
34  /* Global structure containing QuickFit headers
35   *
36   * Each quick list is a skip list of extents, sorted by address in
37   * asceding order.
38   *
39   * Misc lists is a low-height skip list of misc_list structurs, sorted
40   * by range index in ascending order.
41   *
42   * Misc lists themselves are sorted first by size in descending order,
43   * then by address, in ascending order.
```

137

```
44  *
45  * See the algorithm description for the exlanation of the coalesced
46  * flag.
47  */
48  struct qf_allocator{
49      struct skip_list ql[NUM_QUICK_LISTS];
50      struct skip_list mll;
51      bool_t        coalesced;
52      asize_t       free;        // Number of free grains
53  };
54
55  extern struct qf_allocator g_qfalloc;
56
57  /* Comparison function prototypes */
58  int ql_comp(const void *val1, const void *val2);
59  int ml_comp(const void *val1, const void *val2);
60  int mll_comp(const void *val1, const void *val2);
61
62  /* Helper function prototypes */
63  void delete_ext(struct skip_list *list, struct extent *ext, bool_t commit);
64  void store_ext(struct extent *ext, bool_t commit);
65
66  struct skip_list *find_cand_list(const asize_t size);
67  struct extent *find_ext_ql(struct skip_list *candidate, asize_t loc_hint);
68  struct extent *find_ext_ml(struct skip_list *candidate, asize_t loc_hint,
69                              asize_t size);
70
71  inline asize_t mll_range_idx(asize_t size);
72  inline asize_t size_in_grains(asize_t byte_size);
73
74  void split_ext(struct extent *ext, asize_t new_size);
75
76  /* Wrapper functions that call media I/O layer */
77  int write_hdr(struct extent *ext, bool_t is_free);
78  int read_hdr(struct extent *ext);
79
80  /* Parts of the thesis algorithm present in allocator.c */
81  void coalesce(void);
82  void single_alloc(struct skip_list *result,
83                     struct skip_list *candidate, asize_t size,
84                     asize_t loc_hint);
85
86  bool_t multi_alloc(struct skip_list *result, asize_t byte_size,
87                     asize_t loc_hint);
88
89  #endif
```

C.2.8 allocator.c

```
1   #include <assert.h>
2   #include <stdlib.h>
3   #include <stdio.h>
4
5   #include "allocator.h"
6   #include "alloc_exports.h"
7   #include "alloc_stat.h"
8
9   //The declaration of the main allocator structure
10  struct qf_allocator g_qfalloc;
11
12  //The global AWP value
13  unsigned int g_awp;
14  bool_t g_no_coal;
15
16  /*
17   * The task of qf_mkpart is to initialise all free lists, misc_list list
18   * and the wilderness. This function is called once at the start of
19   * the simulation. The partition size provided is in bytes.
20   */
21  void qf_mkpart(uint64_t part_size, unsigned int awp_size, bool_t no_coal){
22      int i;
23      struct extent *ext;
24
25      g_awp = awp_size;
26      g_no_coal = no_coal;
27
28      g_qfalloc.coalesced = TRUE;
29      g_qfalloc.free = 0;
30
31      //Init each quick list
```

138

```
32    for(i = 0; i < NUM_QUICK_LISTS; i++){
33        if(sl_initList(&(g_qfalloc.ql[i]), QL_LEVEL,
34                      MEM_QLISTS, FALSE, &ql_comp) == SL_MEM_EXHAUSTED){
35            errstop("Out_of_memory_in_qf_mkpart", 1);
36        }
37    }
38
39    //Initialise the list of misc lists
40    if(sl_initList(&(g_qfalloc.mll), MLL_LEVEL,
41                   MEM_MLL, FALSE, &mll_comp) == SL_MEM_EXHAUSTED){
42        errstop("Out_of_memory_in_qf_mkpart", 1);
43    }
44
45    //Initialize the misc list, which will contain one or more
46    // 'wilderness' extents.
47    ext = stat_malloc(sizeof(struct extent), MEM_EXTENT);
48    if(ext == NULL){
49        errstop("Out_of_memory_in_qf_mkpart", 1);
50    }
51
52    ext->size = part_size / GRAIN_SIZE;
53    ext->address = 0;
54
55 #ifdef DEBUG
56    fprintf(stderr, "Legend:\tA:_-_Allocate,\n"
57                    "\tF:_-_Free,\n"
58                    "\tC:_-_Coalesce_(+_is_helped;_-_is_no_change),\n"
59                    "\tS_-_Split,\n"
60                    "\tt§_-_Store,\n"
61                    "\ts:_-_single_extent_allocation\n"
62                    "\tm:_-_multi_extent_allocation\n\n\n");
63
64    fprintf(stderr, "Init:_%llu\n", ext->size);
65 #endif
66
67    store_ext(ext, TRUE);
68 }
69
70
71 /*
72  * Implementation of the improved QuickFit allocation algorithm, as
73  * described in the thesis.
74  */
75 struct skip_list *qf_alloc(asize_t byte_size, bool_t cont_hint,
76                            asize_t loc_hint){
77    struct skip_list *candidate = NULL;
78    struct skip_list *result;
79    asize_t grain_size;
80
81 #ifdef DEBUG
82    fprintf(stderr, "A:_%lluB/", byte_size);
83 #endif
84
85    /* Step 0 - Adjust the size, converting it from bytes to grains and
86     * adding one grain if the adjusted size does not fill an exact
87     * number of grains. This re-calculation is used to determine if we
88     * can use single-extent allocation and is passed to single_alloc()
89     * function.
90     */
91    grain_size = size_in_grains(byte_size);
92
93 #ifdef DEBUG
94    fprintf(stderr, "%llug\n", grain_size);
95 #endif
96
97    /* Check if we can possibly satisfy the request. Forward error
98     * correction. The request might still fail if multi-extent
99     * allocation is used.
100    */
101    if(grain_size > g_qfalloc.free){
102        fprintf(stderr, "Out_of_space!_Remaining_grains:_%llu,_needed_%llu\n",
103                g_qfalloc.free, grain_size);
104        return NULL;
105    }
106
107    /* Create and initialise the skipList, which will contain the result
108     * extents. We use the same comparison fanction as the QuickLists,
109     * sorting the extents by address.
110     */
111    result = stat_malloc(sizeof(struct skip_list), MEM_IGNORE);
112    if((result == NULL) ||
113       (sl_initList(result, RES_LEVEL,
114                    MEM_IGNORE, FALSE, &ql_comp) == SL_MEM_EXHAUSTED)){
```

139

```
115        errstop("Out_of_memory_in_qf_alloc!", 2);
116    }
117
118    //Step 1
119    if(cont_hint && !g_qfalloc.coalesced){
120        coalesce();
121    }
122
123    //Step 2 & 3 — locate candidate list
124    candidate = find_cand_list(grain_size);
125
126    //Step 4
127    if((candidate == NULL) && !g_qfalloc.coalesced){
128        coalesce();
129        candidate = find_cand_list(grain_size);
130
131        if(candidate != NULL){
132            as_count_coal_single();
133        }
134
135 #ifdef DEBUG
136        if(candidate != NULL){
137            fprintf(stderr, "C:\t+\n");
138        }else{
139            fprintf(stderr, "C:\t-\n");
140        }
141 #endif
142
143    }else{
144        if(candidate == NULL){
145            as_count_coal_avoided();
146        }
147
148 #ifdef DEBUG
149        if(candidate == NULL){
150            fprintf(stderr, "C:\tesc\n");
151        }
152 #endif
153    }
154
155    //Step 5
156    if(candidate != NULL){ // Allocate from the candidate list
157        single_alloc(result, candidate, grain_size, loc_hint);
158    }else{
159        // Use multi—block allocation, using byte size. If it fails, FALSE
160        // is returned, in wich case, multi_alloc() has emptied and freed
161        // the incomplete results list.
162        if(!multi_alloc(result, byte_size, loc_hint))
163            return NULL;
164    }
165
166    //Print internal fragmentation to file (if activated).
167    as_print_ifrag();
168
169    return result;
170 }
171
172
173 /*
174  * Return all extents from a deleted file to their respective free
175  * lists.
176  */
177 void qf_free(struct skip_list *ext_list){
178    struct extent *ext;
179    statusEnum_t res;
180
181    //The list MUST contain at least one extent.
182    assert(!sl_isEmpty(ext_list));
183
184    /*
185     * Remove extent from the return list one by one and insert them
186     * into the appropriate free lists.
187     */
188    do{
189 #ifdef DEBUG
190        fprintf(stderr, "F:");
191 #endif
192        ext = sl_firstElem(ext_list);
193        sl_delete_node(ext_list, ext, &res);
194        if(res != SL_OK){
195            errstop("Error_deleting_extent_from_return_list!", res);
196        }
197
```

140

```
198      store_ext(ext, TRUE);
199
200      as_sub_from_max_grains(ext->size);
201    }while(!sl_isEmpty(ext_list));
202
203    g_qfalloc.coalesced = FALSE;
204
205    if(!sl_delList(ext_list)){
206      errstop("Failed_to_delete_return_list!", 1);
207    }
208
209    stat_free(ext_list, MEM_IGNORE);
210 }
211
212
213 /*
214  * This function can contain some operations, like statistics
215  * collection, which we want to perform before the allocator
216  * datatstructures are destroyed.
217  */
218 void qf_cleanup(void){
219
220 }
221
222
223 /*
224  * This is the implementation of the coelescing algorithm as described
225  * in the thesis.
226  */
227 void coalesce(void){
228    struct skip_list clist;
229    struct extent *ext, *base_ext, *tmp_ext;
230    struct misc_ext *ml_tmp;
231    int i;
232    statusEnum_t res;
233    bool_t commit;
234    bool_t nomerge = TRUE;
235
236 #ifdef DEBUG
237    fprintf(stderr, "C:\tstart\n");
238 #endif
239
240    /* Define BEAUTIFUL_COALESCING for a visual printout of how many
241     * extents were coalesced and at which positions. Makes for a nice
242     * pattern :)
243     */
244 #ifdef BEAUTIFUL_COALESCING
245    fprintf(stderr, "C:");
246 #endif
247
248    //Do nothing if coalescing was turned off by the driver.
249    if(g_no_coal)
250      return;
251
252    as_count_coal_total();
253
254    /* Create a skiplist, which will hold all in-memory extent headers,
255     * sorted by address (we use ql comparison function). NOT
256     * IMPLEMENTED: The level of coalescing skip list can be determined
257     * dynamically based on the total number of extents in all free
258     * lists, if such a value is maintained.
259     */
260    if(sl_initList(&clist, COAL_LEVEL,
261                   MEM_COAL, FALSE, &ql_comp) == SL_MEM_EXHAUSTED){
262      errstop("Out_of_memory_in_coalesce", 1);
263    }
264
265    /* Traverse all quick lists and move the extents to the coalescing
266     * list, taking care of deleting list_nodes and re-initialising the
267     * ql in the end. Both here and for the misc lists we use
268     * delete_ext() with noCommit flag no set. The changes to the
269     * headers are therefore not written to the disc (when/if that part
270     * is implemented).
271     *
272     * This is basicly an insertion sort, with an improtant difference:
273     * The properties of skip list give us a running time of O(n*log n)
274     */
275    for(i = 0; i < NUM_QUICK_LISTS; i++){
276      while(!sl_isEmpty(&(g_qfalloc.ql[i]))){
277        ext = sl_firstElem(&(g_qfalloc.ql[i]));
278        delete_ext(&(g_qfalloc.ql[i]), ext, FALSE);
279        res = sl_insert_node(&clist, ext);
280        if(res != SL_OK){
```

141

```
281            errstop("Error_inserting_extent_in_coalesce!", res);
282        }
283    }; //while
284  } //for
285
286
287    //Now we do the same for the misc lists
288    while(!sl_isEmpty(&g_qfalloc.mll)){
289
290        //Get the first list on mll. As delete_ext() removes empty misc
291        //lists, the first ml can be different on the next iteration.
292        ml_tmp = sl_firstElem(&(g_qfalloc.mll));
293
294        //Get the first extent on the misc list, and move it to the
295        //coalesce list, not committing on-disk headers.
296        ext = sl_firstElem(&(ml_tmp->extents));
297        delete_ext(&(ml_tmp->extents), ext, FALSE);
298        res = sl_insert_node(&clist, ext);
299        if(res != SL_OK){
300            errstop("Error_inserting_extent_in_coalesce!", res);
301        }
302    }; //while more misc lists on mll
303
304    /* Coalesce the extents and return them to the appropriate free
305     * lists. This on-pass implementation is not fault-tolerant, if the
306     * merged-in headers are cleared on the fly. We need a two-pass
307     * implementation to ensure fault-tolerance, marking the extents as
308     * freed and modified in the first pass, while using the second pass
309     * to write out modified extents _before_ the freed ones are
310     * cleared. That way, if a crash occurs during the second pass, the
311     * integrity of the on-disk headers would be preserved.
312     *
313     * The on-pass implementation is safe to use as long as we do not
314     * clear the on-disk headers of the merged-in extents.
315     */
316
317    base_ext = sl_firstElem(&clist);
318    sl_delete_node(&clist, base_ext, &res);
319    if(res != SL_OK){
320        errstop("Error_emptying_coalesce_list!", res);
321    }
322
323    commit = FALSE;
324    while(!sl_isEmpty(&clist)){
325        tmp_ext = sl_firstElem(&clist);
326        sl_delete_node(&clist, tmp_ext, &res);
327        if(res != SL_OK){
328            errstop("Error_emptying_coalesce_list!", res);
329        }
330
331        if(base_ext->address + base_ext->size == tmp_ext->address){
332            //Adjacent, merge.
333            base_ext->size += tmp_ext->size;
334            commit = TRUE;
335            nomerge = FALSE;
336
337            /* OPTIONAL: Clear the on-disk header of tmp_ext*/
338
339 #ifdef BEAUTIFUL_COALESCING
340            fprintf(stderr, "+");
341 #endif
342
343            stat_free(tmp_ext, MEM_EXTENT);
344        }else{
345            //tmp_ext is not adjacent, flush and forward the base_ext
346            store_ext(base_ext, commit);
347            commit = FALSE;
348            base_ext = tmp_ext;
349
350 #ifdef BEAUTIFUL_COALESCING
351            fprintf(stderr, "_");
352 #endif
353        }
354    };
355    store_ext(base_ext, commit);
356
357    if(nomerge){
358        as_count_coal_nomerge();
359    }
360
361    if(!sl_delList(&clist)){
362        errstop("Failed_to_delete_coalescing_list!", 1);
363    }
```

```
364
365     g_qfalloc.coalesced = TRUE;
366
367  #ifdef BEAUTIFUL_COALESCING
368    fprintf(stderr, "\n");
369  #endif
370  }
371
372
373  /*
374   * Perform the single extent allocation from a free list of any type
375   */
376  void single_alloc(struct skip_list *result,
377                            struct skip_list *candidate, asize_t size,
378                            asize_t loc_hint){
379    struct extent *ext;
380    statusEnum_t res;
381
382    if(((struct extent *)sl_firstElem(candidate))->size <= NUM_QUICK_LISTS){
383      ext = find_ext_ql(candidate, loc_hint);
384    }else{
385      ext = find_ext_ml(candidate, loc_hint, size);
386    }
387
388    if(ext->size > size + g_awp){
389      //Remove the extent from the candidate list. Do not commit header
390      //changes as they will be update in split_ext() anyway
391      delete_ext(candidate, ext, FALSE);
392      split_ext(ext, size);
393    }else{
394      //Remove the extent from the candidate list and commit header changes
395      delete_ext(candidate, ext, TRUE);
396    }
397
398    as_add_to_max_grains(ext->size);
399    as_count_ext();
400
401    res = sl_insert_node(result, ext);
402    if(res == SL_MEM_EXHAUSTED){
403      errstop("Out_of_memory_in_single_alloc!", 2);
404    }
405
406  #ifdef DEBUG
407    fprintf(stderr, "\ts:_%llu\n", ext->size);
408  #endif
409
410  }
411
412
413  /*
414   * Perform a multi-extent allocation. The provided size is in
415   * bytes. The function does its own recalculation to grains for each
416   * new allocated extent.
417   */
418  bool_t multi_alloc(struct skip_list *result, asize_t byte_size,
419                     asize_t loc_hint){
420    //struct list_node *ln_tmp;
421    struct skip_list *candidate = NULL;
422    struct extent *ext;
423    statusEnum_t res;
424    asize_t payload_byte_size, rem_byte_size;
425    bool_t done = FALSE;
426    int i;
427
428    as_count_multiallocs();
429
430    //Initialise the remaining byte size and other variables
431    rem_byte_size = byte_size;
432    ext = NULL;
433
434    do{
435      /* We first check if there is enough free space to go on at the
436       * next iteration. If not, we must return all extents allocated so
437       * far and signal a failure.
438       */
439      if(size_in_grains(rem_byte_size) > g_qfalloc.free){
440        fprintf(stderr, "Out_of_space!_Remaining_grains:_"
441                "%llu,_needed_%llu\n",
442                g_qfalloc.free, size_in_grains(rem_byte_size));
443        qf_free(result);
444
445  #ifdef DEBUG
446        fprintf(stderr, "\tm:_failed\n");
```

143

```
447  #endif
448
449      return FALSE;
450  }
451
452  /* Step 8 */
453
454  /* Check if the list of misc lists is empty. If it is, we can only
455   * allocate from the ql (taking the first non-empty list with the
456   * largest blocks).
457   */
458  if(sl_isEmpty(&(g_qfalloc.mll))){
459      for(i = NUM_QUICK_LISTS - 1; i >= 0; i--){
460          if(!sl_isEmpty(&(g_qfalloc.ql[i]))){
461              candidate = &(g_qfalloc.ql[i]);
462              break;
463          }
464      }
465      ext = find_ext_ql(candidate, loc_hint);
466  }else{
467      //Use the last misc list in mll
468      candidate =
469          &(((struct misc_list *)(g_qfalloc.mll.last->data))->extents);
470
471      //Size 0 — any size will do
472      ext = find_ext_ml(candidate, loc_hint, 0);
473  }
474
475  //Get the number of bytes of payload this extent can contain.
476  payload_byte_size = ext->size * GRAIN_SIZE - HEADER_SIZE;
477
478  /* If the remainder is greater than the payload, subtract the
479   * payload size from the remainder, and do another interation.
480   */
481  if(rem_byte_size > payload_byte_size){
482      rem_byte_size -= payload_byte_size;
483
484      //Remove the extent from the candidate list and commit header
485      //changes.
486      delete_ext(candidate, ext, TRUE);
487
488  }else{ //The extent is the last one in the chain
489
490      //Check if we need to split it.
491      if(ext->size > size_in_grains(rem_byte_size) + g_awp){
492          //Remove the extent from the candidate list. Do not commit
493          //header changes as they will be update in split_ext() anyway
494          delete_ext(candidate, ext, FALSE);
495
496          //Split leaving enough grains to store the remainder
497          split_ext(ext, size_in_grains(rem_byte_size));
498      }else{
499          //Remove the extent from the candidate list and commit header
500          //changes.
501          delete_ext(candidate, ext, TRUE);
502      }
503
504      //Signal stop condition.
505      done = TRUE;
506  }
507
508  //Statistics
509  as_add_to_max_grains(ext->size);
510  as_count_ext();
511
512  //Add the extent to the results list
513  res = sl_insert_node(result, ext);
514  if(res == SL_MEM_EXHAUSTED){
515      errstop("Out_of_memory_in_multi_alloc!", 2);
516  }
517
518  assert(res == SL_OK); //Duplicate key is impossible
519
520  #ifdef DEBUG
521      fprintf(stderr, "\tm:_%llu\n", ext->size);
522  #endif
523
524  }while(!done); /* Step 10 end */
525
526  return TRUE;
527  }
```

144

C.2.9 alloc_helper.c

```
 1  #include <assert.h>
 2  #include <stdlib.h>
 3  #include <stdio.h>
 4
 5  #include "allocator.h"
 6  #include "alloc_stat.h"
 7  #include "media.h"
 8
 9  //#define STAT_USE
10
11
12  /**************** Allocator Helper Functions ******************/
13
14
15  /*
16   * Delete the extent from the free list. If the extent was the last
17   * one in a misc list, the delete that misc list from mll. The caller
18   * is responsible for freeing the extent itself.
19   */
20  void delete_ext(struct skip_list *list, struct extent *ext, bool_t commit){
21      struct extent *tmp;
22      struct misc_list dummy, *ml_tmp;
23      statusEnum_t res;
24
25      //Delete the extent from the list.
26      tmp = sl_delete_node(list, ext, &res);
27      assert(res == SL_OK);
28      assert(ext == tmp);
29
30      //If it was the last extent in a misc list, delete the misc list
31      //from mll.
32      if((ext->size > NUM_QUICK_LISTS) && sl_isEmpty(list)){
33          dummy.range_idx = mll_range_idx(ext->size);
34          ml_tmp = sl_delete_node(&(g_qfalloc.mll), &dummy, &res);
35
36          if(res != SL_OK)
37              errstop("List_error_in_delete_ext!", res);
38          assert(res == SL_OK);
39
40          if(!sl_delList(&(ml_tmp->extents))){
41              errstop("Failed_to_delete_misc_list!", 1);
42          }
43
44          stat_free(ml_tmp, MEM_MLISTS);
45      }
46
47      /* If the extent was not deleted for the sake of coalescing, write
48       * its header down to disk and mark it as 'used'.
49       */
50      if(commit){
51          write_hdr(ext, FALSE);
52      }
53
54      g_qfalloc.free -= ext->size;
55
56      as_print_pool_use(g_qfalloc.free, ext->size, FALSE);
57  }
58
59
60  /*
61   * This function stores an extent in an appropriate free list. It
62   * first decides if an extent belongs to a quick list. If it is so, an
63   * insert function call is performed. If the extent belongs to a misc
64   * list, the function first checks if the the appropriate misc list
65   * exists. If not, it first creates the header for that list and then
66   * inserts the extent in the misc list.
67   */
68  void store_ext(struct extent *ext, bool_t commit){
69      statusEnum_t res;
70      struct misc_list dummy;
71      struct misc_list *tmp;
72
73  #ifdef DEBUG
74      fprintf(stderr, "\t#_%llu\n", ext->size);
75  #endif
76
77      //Check if the extent belongs to a quick list
78      if(ext->size <= NUM_QUICK_LISTS){
79          sl_insert_node(&(g_qfalloc.ql[ext->size - 1]), ext);
80      }else{
```

145

```
81      //It is a misc list, then. We first check if the appropriate misc
82      //list exists.
83      dummy.range_idx = mll_range_idx(ext->size);
84      tmp = sl_find_node(&(g_qfalloc.mll), &dummy, &res);
85      if(res == SL_MEM_EXHAUSTED){
86          errstop("Out_of_memory_in_store_ext!", 1);
87      }
88
89      //Create new misc list if it is not already present.
90      if(res != SL_OK){
91          tmp = stat_malloc(sizeof(struct misc_list), MEM_MLISTS);
92          if((tmp == NULL) ||
93             ((sl_initList(&(tmp->extents), ML_LEVEL, MEM_MLISTS, FALSE,
94                      &ml_comp) == SL_MEM_EXHAUSTED))){
95              errstop("Out_of_memory:_Cannot_create_misc_list", 1);
96          }
97          tmp->range_idx = mll_range_idx(ext->size);
98
99          //Insert the misc list into the list of the misc lists
100         if(sl_insert_node(&(g_qfalloc.mll), tmp) != SL_OK){
101             errstop("Fatal_error_in_sl_inser_node", res);
102         }
103     }
104
105     //We can now insert an extent into the misc list.
106     if(sl_insert_node(&(tmp->extents), ext) != SL_OK){
107         errstop("Fatal_error_in_sl_inser_node", res);
108     }
109 }
110
111 //Commit the extent header to disk and mark it as 'free'.
112 if(commit){
113     write_hdr(ext, TRUE);
114 }
115
116 //Update the free space counter
117 g_qfalloc.free += ext->size;
118
119 as_print_pool_use(g_qfalloc.free, ext->size, TRUE);
120 }
121
122
123
124
125 /*
126  * Find a candidate free list, which might contain an extent of
127  * desired size.
128  */
129 struct skip_list *find_cand_list(const asize_t size){
130     struct skip_list *candidate = NULL;
131     struct misc_list dummy, *ml;
132     struct list_node *mll_node;
133     struct extent *ext;
134     asize_t cand_size;
135     statusEnum_t res;
136
137     cand_size = size;
138
139     /* First we go through all quick lists, stating with the given index */
140     while(cand_size <= NUM_QUICK_LISTS){
141         candidate = &(g_qfalloc.ql[cand_size - 1]);
142         assert(candidate != NULL); //Cannot have uninitialised ql's
143
144         //If the list is empty, try the next one (can happen for ql)
145         if(sl_isEmpty(candidate)){
146             cand_size++;
147         }else{
148             return candidate; // Otherwise make an early exit :)
149         }
150     };
151
152     /* No candidate found among ql's, search ml's */
153
154     /*
155      * We do a raw misc list search. First we use a specially modified
156      * SkipList find function to locate the first misc list, which range
157      * is greater or equal to the cand_size.
158      *
159      * From there on we examine the last extent in each subsequent misc
160      * list, starting with the returned ml_node. We return the
161      * misc_list, which contains an extent with size >= 'size'
162      * parameter. By the sorting invariant for misc lists, the last
163      * extent is the largest one.
```

```
164    */
165
166    // Locate the first non-empty list_node
167    dummy.range_idx = mll_range_idx(cand_size);
168    mll_node = sl_find_listnode(&(g_qfalloc.mll), &dummy, &res);
169
170    // Check if no suitable misc lists found
171    if(res == SL_PAST_LAST_NODE){
172      return NULL;
173    }
174
175    /* From here, traverse mll node for node. If the misc list provided
176     * by sl_find_listnode() does not contain extents of desired size,
177     * the next list will. The code in while() is executed at most two
178     * times.
179     */
180    while(mll_node != g_qfalloc.mll.nil){
181      ml = (struct misc_list *)(mll_node->data);
182      candidate = &(ml->extents);
183
184      //Verify invariant: empty misc lists are deleted from mll
185      assert(!sl_isEmpty(candidate));
186
187      //Check the size inequity and return if matches
188      ext = candidate->last->data;
189      if(ext->size >= size){
190        return candidate;
191      }
192
193      //Advance to the next misc list in mll skip_list
194      mll_node = mll_node->forward[0];
195    };
196
197    return NULL;
198  }
199
200
201
202  /*
203   * This function finds a required extent from a quick list, based on
204   * the provided size and locality information. This function is used
205   * both by single_alloc() and multi_alloc()
206   */
207  struct extent *find_ext_ql(struct skip_list *candidate, asize_t loc_hint){
208    struct extent *ext = NULL;
209    struct extent dummy;
210    statusEnum_t res;
211
212    assert(candidate != NULL);
213    assert(!sl_isEmpty(candidate));
214    assert(((struct extent *)sl_firstElem(candidate))->size <=
215           NUM_QUICK_LISTS);
216
217    /* Without the locality hint get the first extent on the quick list,
218     * otherwise do an address search, getting the extent which address
219     * is >= loc_hint.
220     */
221    if(loc_hint == 0){
222      ext = sl_firstElem(candidate);
223    }else{
224      dummy.address = loc_hint;
225      ext = sl_find_node(candidate, &dummy, &res);
226      if(res == SL_PAST_LAST_NODE){
227        ext = candidate->last->data;
228      }
229    }
230
231    return ext;
232  }
233
234
235  /*
236   * This function finds a required extent from a misc list, based on
237   * the provided size and locality information. This function is used
238   * both by single_alloc() and multi_alloc()
239   */
240  struct extent *find_ext_ml(struct skip_list *candidate, asize_t loc_hint,
241                             asize_t size){
242    struct list_node *ln_tmp;
243    struct extent *ext = NULL, *best_ext;
244    struct extent dummy;
245    asize_t best_val;
246    statusEnum_t res;
```

147

```
247
248     assert(candidate != NULL);
249     assert(!sl_isEmpty(candidate));
250     assert(((struct extent *)sl_firstElem(candidate))->size >
251             NUM_QUICK_LISTS);
252
253     /* Without the locality hint: If the size value is 0, the function
254      * is called from multi_alloc(), in which case get the largest
255      * extent on the misc list (which is the last one), otherwise do a
256      * best fit search on the misc list.
257      */
258     if(loc_hint == 0){
259        if(size == 0){
260           ext = candidate->last->data;
261        }else{
262           dummy.size = size;
263           dummy.address = 0;
264           ext = sl_find_node(candidate, &dummy, &res);
265           if(res == SL_PAST_LAST_NODE){
266              ext = candidate->last->data;
267           }
268        }
269     }else{
270        /* We quickly locate the first _list node_ which contents is
271         * suitable. From there we search the list for the closest
272         * locality address. With size == 0 we will implicitly start from
273         * the first node with the best locality.
274         */
275        dummy.size = size;
276        dummy.address = loc_hint;
277        ln_tmp = sl_find_listnode(candidate, &dummy, &res);
278        if(res == SL_PAST_LAST_NODE){
279           ln_tmp = candidate->last;
280        }
281
282        //Seach the remaining nodes for the address, with the shortest
283        //distance from loc_hint.
284        best_ext = ln_tmp->data;
285        best_val = best_ext->address - loc_hint;
286
287        while(ln_tmp->forward[0] != candidate->nil){
288           ext = ln_tmp->data;
289
290           if(ext->address - loc_hint < best_val){
291              best_ext = ext;
292              best_val = ext->address - loc_hint;
293           }
294
295           if(best_val == 0)
296              break;
297
298           ln_tmp = ln_tmp->forward[0];
299        };
300        ext = best_ext;
301     }
302
303     return ext;
304  }
305
306
307
308  /*
309   * This function splits the supplied extent, reducing it to the given
310   * size and returning the remainder to the appropriate free list.
311   */
312  void split_ext(struct extent *ext, asize_t new_size){
313     struct extent *tmp;
314
315     assert(new_size < ext->size);
316
317  #ifdef DEBUG
318     fprintf(stderr, "\t8\n");
319  #endif
320
321     tmp = stat_malloc(sizeof(struct extent), MEM_EXTENT);
322     if(tmp == NULL){
323        errstop("Out_of_memory:_Cannot_create_new_extent_during_split", 1);
324     }
325
326     tmp->size = ext->size - new_size;
327     tmp->address = ext->address + new_size;
328
329     store_ext(tmp, TRUE);
```

```
330
331      ext->size = new_size;
332
333      //Update the on-disk header with the new size value and mark it as
334      //'not free'.
335      write_hdr(ext, FALSE);
336  }
337
338
339
340  /************************
341   * Comparison functions *
342   ************************/
343
344  /* Comparison function for the entries in a quick list */
345  int ql_comp(const void *val1, const void *val2){
346      if(((struct extent *)val1)->address > ((struct extent *)val2)->address)
347          return 1;
348
349      if(((struct extent *)val1)->address < ((struct extent *)val2)->address)
350          return -1;
351
352      return 0;
353  }
354
355  /* Comparison function for the entries in a misc list */
356  int ml_comp(const void *val1, const void *val2){
357      const struct extent *m1 = (struct extent *)val1;
358      const struct extent *m2 = (struct extent *)val2;
359
360      if(m1->size > m2->size)
361          return 1;
362
363      if(m1->size < m2->size)
364          return -1;
365
366      //If the sizes are equal, then we sort by address. Both values in
367      //ascending order.
368      if(m1->size == m2->size){
369          if(m1->address > m2->address)
370              return 1;
371
372          if(m1->address < m2->address)
373              return -1;
374      } // if sizes are equal
375
376      return 0;
377  }
378
379  /* Comparison function for the entries in a list of misc lists */
380  int mll_comp(const void *val1, const void *val2){
381      if(((struct misc_list *)val1)->range_idx >
382         ((struct misc_list *)val2)->range_idx)
383          return 1;
384
385      if(((struct misc_list *)val1)->range_idx <
386         ((struct misc_list *)val2)->range_idx)
387          return -1;
388
389      return 0;
390  }
391
392
393
394  /* Calculate to which misc list an extent of given size belongs. */
395  inline asize_t mll_range_idx(asize_t size){
396      assert(size > NUM_QUICK_LISTS);
397      return (size - NUM_QUICK_LISTS) / MISC_RANGE;
398  }
399
400
401  /*
402   * Calculate how many grains are need to accomodate the given number
403   * of bytes, should everything fit into a single extent.
404   */
405  inline asize_t size_in_grains(asize_t byte_size){
406      return (byte_size + HEADER_SIZE) / GRAIN_SIZE +
407          ((((byte_size + HEADER_SIZE) % GRAIN_SIZE) == 0) ? 0 : 1);
408  }
409
410
411  /*
412   * The function updates the on-disk header, writing out the size and
```

149

```
413  * the allocation status.
414  */
415  int write_hdr(struct extent *ext, bool_t is_free){
416      asize_t header;
417
418      //We scramble the header and then write it out
419      header = ext->size | ((asize_t)is_free << (sizeof(asize_t) * 8 - 1));
420
421      put_range(ext, 0, HEADER_SIZE, &header, TRUE);
422
423      return 0;
424  }
425
426
427
428  /*
429   * ext parameter provides the address from which the extent header is
430   * to be read. The information is read to a temporary buffer. It is
431   * then discrambled and copied to the extent parameter (the last step
432   * is not implemented in this simulation).
433   */
434  int read_hdr(struct extent *ext){
435      asize_t header;
436
437      get_range(ext, 0, HEADER_SIZE, &header);
438
439      /* Discramble and copy, possibly returning the free status as part of
440       * the return value. NOT IMPLEMENTED.
441       */
442
443      return 0;
444  }
```

C.2.10 media.h

```
1   #ifndef MEDIA_H
2   #define MEDIA_H
3
4   #include "common.h"
5
6   extern uint64_t g_read_count, g_write_count;
7
8   /*
9    * Stub functions for the media I/O layer.
10   */
11
12  void mediaInit(void);
13  int put_range(const struct extent *ext, asize_t offset,
14                  asize_t length, void *data, bool_t destructive);
15  int get_range(const struct extent *ext, asize_t offset,
16                  asize_t length, void *data);
17
18  #endif
```

C.2.11 media.c

```
1   #include <stdio.h>
2   #include <stdlib.h>
3
4   #include "media.h"
5
6   uint64_t g_read_count, g_write_count;
7
8   void mediaInit(void){
9       g_read_count = g_write_count = 0;
10  }
11
12
13  /*
14   * Extent header in the first parameter provide extent's starting
15   * address. Extent's size can be used for sanity check.
16   */
17  int put_range(const struct extent *ext, asize_t offset,
18                  asize_t length, void *data, bool_t destructive){
19
20      /* Check if wee need to fetch a grain to preserve its
21       * contents. Between zero and two read operations might be needed,
```

150

```
22      * depending on the alignment of data.
23      */
24      if(!destructive){
25        get_range(ext, offset, length, data);
26      }
27
28      g_write_count++;
29      return 0;
30  }
31  }
32
33
34  int get_range(const struct extent *ext, asize_t offset,
35                asize_t length, void *data){
36
37      g_read_count++;
38      return 0;
39  }
```

C.2.12   memory.h

```
1   #ifndef MEMORY_H
2   #define MEMORY_H
3
4   /* Wrapper function for malloc and free intended to measure memory
5    * consumption of the various parts of the allocator.*
6    */
7
8   typedef enum {
9     MEM_IGNORE,      //All skip lists are traced by default. This class is
10                     //used if we want to disable tracing.
11    MEM_MLL,         //The list of misc lists
12    MEM_QLISTS,      //Quick lists
13    MEM_MLISTS,      //Misc lists
14    MEM_EXTENT,      //In-memory extent headers
15    MEM_COAL,        //Coalescing master list
16  } memstat_t;
17
18
19  //Total number of entries in memstat_t
20  #define MEM_LAST 6
21
22  void stat_mem_init(void);
23  void stat_mem_print(void);
24  void *stat_malloc(size_t size, memstat_t infotype);
25  void stat_free(void *ptr, memstat_t infotype);
26
27  #endif
```

C.2.13   memory.c

```
1   #include <stdlib.h>
2   #include <stdint.h>
3   #include <stdio.h>
4   #include <string.h>
5   #include <malloc.h>
6
7   #include "memory.h"
8   #include "skiplist.h"
9
10  //Undefine this to exclude memory usage statistics collection.
11  //#define STAT_MEMORY
12
13  //Undefine to avoid writing memory allocation/deallocation to the
14  //respective files.
15  //#define STAT_MEM_FILE
16
17  //This is used to keep track of the allocated memory sizes
18  struct skip_list g_mem_list;
19
20  struct mem_data{
21    size_t size;
22    void *ptr;
23  };
24
25  struct meminfo{
26    uint64_t running;
```

151

```
27    uint64_t max;
28    uint64_t total;
29    FILE *memory_file;
30  };
31
32  char *g_statnames[MEM_LAST] = {"ignored",
33                                 "misclist_list",
34                                 "quick_lists",
35                                 "misc_lists",
36                                 "extent_headers",
37                                 "coalescing_list"};
38
39  struct meminfo g_meminfo[MEM_LAST];
40
41  uint64_t g_access_count;
42  uint64_t g_running, g_max, g_total; //Used for cumulative usage
43
44
45  /* Comparison function for memory module, ordering the entries by
46   * address.
47   */
48  int mem_comp(const void *val1, const void *val2){
49    if(((struct mem_data *)val1)->ptr > ((struct mem_data *)val2)->ptr)
50      return 1;
51
52    if(((struct mem_data *)val1)->ptr < ((struct mem_data *)val2)->ptr)
53      return -1;
54
55    return 0;
56  }
57
58
59  /* Initialise all memory tracking tructures */
60  void stat_mem_init(void){
61  #ifdef STAT_MEMORY
62    statusEnum_t res;
63
64    memset(g_meminfo, 0, sizeof(struct meminfo) * MEM_LAST);
65
66    g_access_count = 0;
67    g_running = g_max = g_total = 0;
68
69  #ifdef STAT_MEM_FILE
70    char tmp[256];
71
72    //Starting count from 1 - MEM_IGNORE excluded
73    for(int i = 1; i < MEM_LAST; i++){
74      sprintf(tmp, "%s.mem", g_statnames[i]);
75      g_meminfo[i].memory_file = fopen(tmp, "w");
76    }
77  #endif //STAT_MEM_FILE
78
79    //Must be called at the very end of initialisation
80    res = sl_initList(&g_mem_list, 38, MEM_IGNORE, FALSE, &mem_comp);
81    if(res != SL_OK){
82      errstop("Memory_module_failed!\n", res);
83    }
84
85  #endif //STAT_MEMORY
86  }
87
88
89  /* Print the collected statistics */
90  void stat_mem_print(void){
91  #ifdef STAT_MEMORY
92    int i;
93
94    fprintf(stderr, "\n***_Memory_usage_***\n\n");
95
96    fprintf(stderr, "Total_access_count:_%llu\n", g_access_count);
97    fprintf(stderr, "Total_usage_hight_watermark:_%llu\n", g_max);
98    fprintf(stderr, "Total_usage_throughput:_%llu\n\n", g_total);
99
100
101   //Starting count from 1 - MEM_IGNORE excluded
102   for(i = 1; i < MEM_LAST; i++){
103     fprintf(stderr, "%s_high_watermark:_%llu\n",
104             g_statnames[i], g_meminfo[i].max);
105     fprintf(stderr, "%s_throughput:_%llu\n",
106             g_statnames[i], g_meminfo[i].total);
107   }
108 #endif
109 }
```

152

```
110
111
112
113  void *stat_malloc(size_t size, memstat_t infotype){
114  #ifdef STAT_MEMORY
115    void *tmp;
116    struct mem_data *md;
117    statusEnum_t res;
118
119    tmp = malloc(size);
120
121    //Prevent recursion
122    if(infotype != MEM_IGNORE){
123      if((md = malloc(sizeof(struct mem_data))) == NULL){
124        errstop("Memory_module_failed!\n", 99);
125      }
126
127      md->size = size;
128      md->ptr = tmp;
129      res = sl_insert_node(&g_mem_list, md);
130      if(res != SL_OK){
131        errstop("Memory_module_failed!\n", res);
132      }
133
134      g_access_count++;
135      g_running += size;
136      g_total += size;
137      g_meminfo[infotype].running += size; //malloc_usable_size(tmp);
138      g_meminfo[infotype].total += size;   //malloc_usable_size(tmp);
139
140  #ifdef STAT_MEM_FILE
141      fprintf(g_meminfo[infotype].memory_file, "%llu\t%llu\n",
142              g_access_count, g_meminfo[infotype].running);
143  #endif //STAT_MEM_FILE
144
145      if(g_running > g_max)
146        g_max = g_running;
147
148      if(g_meminfo[infotype].running > g_meminfo[infotype].max)
149        g_meminfo[infotype].max = g_meminfo[infotype].running;
150    }
151
152    return tmp;
153  #else
154    return malloc(size);
155  #endif
156  }
157
158
159  void stat_free(void *ptr, memstat_t infotype){
160  #ifdef STAT_MEMORY
161    struct mem_data *md, dummy;
162    statusEnum_t res;
163
164    //Prevent recursion
165    if(infotype != MEM_IGNORE){
166      dummy.ptr = ptr;
167      md = sl_delete_node(&g_mem_list, &dummy, &res);
168      if(res != SL_OK){
169        errstop("Memory_module_failed!\n", res);
170      }
171
172      g_access_count++;
173      g_running -= md->size;
174      g_meminfo[infotype].running -= md->size; //malloc_usable_size(ptr);
175
176      free(md);
177
178  #ifdef STAT_MEM_FILE
179      fprintf(g_meminfo[infotype].memory_file, "%llu\t%llu\n",
180              g_access_count, g_meminfo[infotype].running);
181  #endif //STAT_MEM_FILE
182    }
183
184  #endif //STAT_MEMORY
185    free(ptr);
186  }
```

C.2.14 alloc_stat.h

```
1  #ifndef ALLOC_STAT_H
```

```c
2   #define ALLOC_STAT_H
3
4   #include "common.h" //For asize_t
5
6   void as_init(void);
7
8   void as_add_to_max_grains(asize_t grains);
9   void as_sub_from_max_grains(asize_t grains);
10  uint64_t as_get_max_grains(void);
11
12  void as_count_ext(void);
13  uint64_t as_get_ext_count(void);
14  void as_count_files(void);
15  uint64_t as_get_file_count(void);
16  long double as_get_ffrag_avg(void);
17  long double as_get_ffrag_max(void);
18
19  void as_print_pool_use(asize_t free, asize_t diff, bool_t op);
20
21  void as_count_coal_total(void);
22  void as_count_coal_single(void);
23  void as_count_coal_nomerge(void);
24  void as_count_coal_avoided(void);
25  void as_get_coal_status(int *total, int *single, int *avoided,
26                          int *nomerge);
27
28  void as_add_to_max_bytes(asize_t bytes);
29  void as_sub_from_max_bytes(asize_t bytes);
30  uint64_t as_get_max_bytes(void);
31  long double as_get_ifrag_avg(void);
32
33  void as_print_ifrag(void);
34
35  void as_count_multiallocs(void);
36  asize_t as_get_multiallocs(void);
37
38  #endif
```

C.2.15 alloc_stat.c

```c
1   #include <stdlib.h>
2   #include <stdio.h>
3   #include <string.h>
4   #include <stdint.h>
5
6   #include "alloc_stat.h"
7   #include "allocator.h"
8
9   struct astat{
10      asize_t grains_running;
11      asize_t grains_max;
12      asize_t ext_count;
13      asize_t file_count;
14      FILE *pool;
15      int coal_total;
16      int coal_single;
17      int coal_avoided;
18      int coal_nomerge;
19      FILE *ifrag;
20      asize_t bytes_running;
21      asize_t bytes_max;
22      asize_t multi_allocs;
23      long double ffrag_max;
24  };
25
26
27  struct astat g_alloc_stat;
28
29
30  void as_init(void){
31      bzero(&g_alloc_stat, sizeof(struct astat));
32
33  #ifdef POOL_USE
34      g_alloc_stat.pool = fopen("free_pool.stat", "w");
35  #endif
36
37  #ifdef IFRAG
38      g_alloc_stat.ifrag = fopen("internal_frag.stat", "w");
39  #endif
40  }
```

```
41
42
43
44   /** Count the allocated grains **/
45
46   void as_add_to_max_grains(asize_t grains){
47     g_alloc_stat.grains_running += grains;
48
49     if(g_alloc_stat.grains_running > g_alloc_stat.grains_max)
50       g_alloc_stat.grains_max = g_alloc_stat.grains_running;
51
52   }
53
54   void as_sub_from_max_grains(asize_t grains){
55     g_alloc_stat.grains_running -= grains;
56   }
57
58   uint64_t as_get_max_grains(void){
59     return g_alloc_stat.grains_max;
60   }
61
62
63
64   /** Statistics of File Fragmentation **/
65
66   void as_count_ext(void){
67     long double tmp;
68
69     g_alloc_stat.ext_count++;
70
71     //Recalculate maximum file fragmentation. File count is updated from
72     //the simulation driver prior to any call to this function.
73     tmp = (long double) g_alloc_stat.ext_count /
74       (long double) g_alloc_stat.file_count;
75
76     if(tmp > g_alloc_stat.ffrag_max)
77       g_alloc_stat.ffrag_max = tmp;
78   }
79
80   uint64_t as_get_ext_count(void){
81     return g_alloc_stat.ext_count;
82   }
83
84   void as_count_files(void){
85     g_alloc_stat.file_count++;
86   }
87
88   uint64_t as_get_file_count(void){
89     return g_alloc_stat.file_count;
90   }
91
92   long double as_get_ffrag_avg(void){
93     return (long double) g_alloc_stat.ext_count /
94       (long double) g_alloc_stat.file_count;
95   }
96
97   long double as_get_ffrag_max(void){
98     return g_alloc_stat.ffrag_max;
99   }
100
101
102
103  /** If activated, dump free pool status to file. **/
104  void as_print_pool_use(asize_t free, asize_t size, bool_t op){
105  #ifdef POOL_USE
106      fprintf(g_alloc_stat.pool, "%llu\t%c\t%llu\n",
107              free, op ? '+' : '-', size);
108  #endif
109  }
110
111
112
113  /** A set of functions counting coalescings **/
114  void as_count_coal_total(void){
115    g_alloc_stat.coal_total++;
116  }
117
118  void as_count_coal_single(void){
119    g_alloc_stat.coal_single++;
120  }
121
122  void as_count_coal_nomerge(void){
123    g_alloc_stat.coal_nomerge++;
```

155

```
124 }
125
126 void as_count_coal_avoided(void){
127     g_alloc_stat.coal_avoided++;
128 }
129
130 void as_get_coal_status(int *total, int *single, int *avoided,
131                                     int *nomerge){
132     *total = g_alloc_stat.coal_total;
133     *single = g_alloc_stat.coal_single;
134     *avoided = g_alloc_stat.coal_avoided;
135     *nomerge = g_alloc_stat.coal_nomerge;
136 }
137
138
139
140 /** Statistics of Internal Fragmentation **/
141
142 void as_add_to_max_bytes(asize_t bytes){
143     g_alloc_stat.bytes_running += bytes;
144
145     if(g_alloc_stat.bytes_running > g_alloc_stat.bytes_max)
146         g_alloc_stat.bytes_max = g_alloc_stat.bytes_running;
147
148 }
149
150 void as_sub_from_max_bytes(asize_t bytes){
151     g_alloc_stat.bytes_running -= bytes;
152 }
153
154 uint64_t as_get_max_bytes(void){
155     return g_alloc_stat.bytes_max;
156 }
157
158
159 long double as_get_ifrag_avg(void){
160     return ((long double)g_alloc_stat.grains_max * GRAIN_SIZE) /
161         (long double)g_alloc_stat.bytes_max;
162 }
163
164
165 /**
166     Collect and dump to file running internal fragmentation
167     statistics
168 **/
169 void as_print_ifrag(void){
170 #ifdef IFRAG
171     fprintf(g_alloc_stat.ifrag, "%.8Lf\n",
172                 ((long double)g_alloc_stat.grains_running * GRAIN_SIZE) /
173                 (long double)g_alloc_stat.bytes_running);
174 #endif
175 }
176
177
178
179 /**
180     Count the allocation requests that had to be split over several
181     extents
182 **/
183
184 void as_count_multiallocs(void){
185     g_alloc_stat.multi_allocs++;
186 }
187
188 asize_t as_get_multiallocs(void){
189     return g_alloc_stat.multi_allocs;
190 }
```

C.2.16 Makefile

```
 1 CC_OPTS = -O3 -Wall
 2 LD_OPTS = -O3
 3 LIBS = simalloc.o memory.o allocator.o skiplist.o \
 4     alloc_helper.o alloc_stat.o media.o libarg.o
 5 PROG = simalloc
 6
 7 # Uncomment the first line to collect memory usage information
 8 # Uncomment both lines to additionally dump memory usage dynamics
 9 # to file
10 MEMSTAT = -DSTAT_MEMORY
```

156

```
11  #MEMSTAT += -DSTAT_MEM_FILE -std=c99
12
13  # Uncomment the following line to print the running status of free
14  # space pool to file.
15  #STAT_OPTS = -DPOOL_USE
16
17  # Uncomment the following line to print the running status of internal
18  # fragmentation (in percent). IFRAG and POLL_USE can be used at the
19  # same time or individually.
20  #STAT_OPTS += -DIFRAG
21
22  # Uncomment the following line to print the operations performed by
23  # the allocator to stderr in a human-readable format (debug
24  # information).
25  #CC_OPTS += -DDEBUG
26
27  .PHONY: all clean realclean
28
29  all: $(PROG)
30
31  clean:
32          rm -f *.o *~
33
34  realclean: clean
35          rm -f $(PROG) $(PROG).exe
36          rm -f *.stackdump core
37
38
39  simalloc: $(LIBS)
40          gcc $(LD_OPTS) -o $@ $(LIBS)
41
42  simalloc.o: simalloc.c ../common/storage_types.h simalloc.h \
43          alloc_exports.h memory.h skiplist.h common.h media.h \
44          ../common/libarg.h alloc_stat.h
45          gcc $(CC_OPTS) -c $<
46
47  allocator.o: allocator.c memory.h allocator.h alloc_exports.h \
48          common.h skiplist.h alloc_stat.h
49          gcc $(CC_OPTS) -c $<
50
51  alloc_helper.o: alloc_helper.c memory.h allocator.h common.h \
52          skiplist.h media.h alloc_stat.h
53          gcc $(CC_OPTS) -c $<
54
55  alloc_stat.o: alloc_stat.c alloc_stat.h common.h
56          gcc $(CC_OPTS) $(STAT_OPTS) -c $<
57
58  memory.o: memory.c memory.h
59          gcc $(CC_OPTS) $(MEMSTAT) -c $<
60
61  skiplist.o: skiplist.c skiplist.h memory.h common.h
62          gcc $(CC_OPTS) -c $<
63
64  media.o: media.c media.h common.h
65          gcc $(CC_OPTS) -c $<
66
67  libarg.o: ../common/libarg.c ../common/libarg.h
68          gcc $(CC_OPTS) -c $<
```

C.3 Trace Generator

The trace generator has two main programs. `clean_trace.cc` parses the binary HTTP and Helix server logs and generates a temporary merged log, filtering the entries which are not relevant for the purpose of our simulation. `mkalloctrc.c` then read the temporary cleaned log and generates a trace of allocation and deallocation events as described in Appendix B. `print_repl.cc` parses the binary replacement log produced by `mkalloctrc.c` and prints it in text form, optionally showing the URL strings.

C.3.1 client_event.h

Only two structures are used from client_event.h. These structures describe each entry of the raw binary HTTP and Helix server logs. These logs are parsed to generate our allocation trace.

```
 1  struct http_event {
 2      double                  abstime;        // local time!
 3      unsigned char   url[8];
 4      unsigned int    client_ip;
 5      unsigned int    protocol;
 6      unsigned int    bytes_sent;
 7      unsigned int    session_id;
 8      unsigned short  method;
 9      unsigned short  status;
10      unsigned short  session_state;
11      unsigned short  unused;
12  } __attribute__((packed));
13
14  struct helix_event {
15      http_event              http;
16      unsigned int    file_size;
17      float                       file_time;
18      float                       time_sent;
19      float                       elapsed_time;
20  } __attribute__((packed));
21
22  #define ST_STAT(st)     (st & 0xFFF)
```

C.3.2 clean_trace.cc

```
 1  #include "../scripts/client_event.h"
 2  #include "../scripts/stt/stage_bdb_map.h"
 3  #include "assert.h"
 4  #include <stdio.h>
 5  #include <stdlib.h>
 6  #include <string.h>
 7  #include <limits.h>
 8
 9  #include "../common/storage_types.h"
10  #include "../common/libarg.h"
11
12  #define TIME_MAX_VAL ((double)LONG_MAX * (double)1000)
13
14  inline int isValidURL(const char *url){
15    if(url[strlen(url) - 1] == '?')
16      return 1;
17    else
```

```
18      return 0;
19  }
20
21  int main(int argc, char **argv){
22    struct http_event ht_ev;
23    struct helix_event hx_ev;
24    struct raw_trace rt;
25    FILE *ht_file, *hx_file, *out_file;
26    char *param;
27    unsigned long long invalid_count, status_count, total_count;
28
29    invalid_count = status_count = total_count = 0;
30
31    /* Parse the arguements */
32    ht_file = hx_file = out_file = NULL;
33
34    if(parseArgs(argc, argv, "-t", FALSE, &param) && (param != NULL)){
35      if((ht_file = fopen(param, "r")) == NULL){
36        printf("Cannot open binary http trace!\n");
37        return 1;
38      }
39    }
40
41    if(parseArgs(argc, argv, "-x", FALSE, &param) && (param != NULL)){
42      if((hx_file = fopen(param, "r")) == NULL){
43        printf("Cannot open binary helix trace!\n");
44        return 1;
45      }
46    }
47
48    if(parseArgs(argc, argv, "-o", FALSE, &param) && (param != NULL)){
49      if((out_file = fopen(param, "w")) == NULL){
50        printf("Cannot open output file!\n");
51        return 1;
52      }
53    }
54
55    /* Must be the last arg check as param value is used later */
56    parseArgs(argc, argv, "-d", FALSE, &param);
57
58    if((param == NULL) ||
59       (out_file == NULL) ||
60       ((ht_file == NULL) && (hx_file == NULL))){
61      printf("Usage:\n%s [-t http_trace | -x helix_trace | both]"
62             " -d hash_db -o out_trace\n", argv[0]);
63      return 1;
64    }
65
66    /* Open the URL database. */
67    bdb db(param, DB_UNKNOWN, DB_RDONLY);
68    bdb_map<url_key, char*> hash_url(db);
69
70    //Initialise the times with maximum possible values for the benifit
71    //of comparison in the case when we read only one file.
72    ht_ev.abstime = hx_ev.http.abstime = TIME_MAX_VAL;
73
74
75    /* Read the first entries of both input files*/
76    if(ht_file != NULL){
77      if(fread(&ht_ev, sizeof(struct http_event), 1, ht_file) != 1){
78        printf("Empty file?\n");
79        return 1;
80      }
81      total_count++;
82    }
83
84    if(hx_file != NULL){
85      if(fread(&hx_ev, sizeof(struct helix_event), 1, hx_file) != 1){
86        printf("Empty file?\n");
87        return 1;
88      }
89      total_count++;
90    }
91
92    /* The main processing loop */
93    for(;;){
94      //Compare times of the two events an prepare for output the
95      //earliest one.
96      if(ht_ev.abstime < hx_ev.http.abstime){
97        rt.bytes_sent = ht_ev.bytes_sent;
98        rt.status = ST_STAT(ht_ev.status);
99        memcpy((char *)rt.url, (const char *)ht_ev.url, 8);
100
```

159

```
101        /* Read the next http event*/
102        if(fread(&ht_ev, sizeof(struct http_event), 1, ht_file) != 1){
103          /* Reset the impoortant structures if EOF reached*/
104          fclose(ht_file);
105          ht_file = NULL;
106          ht_ev.abstime = TIME_MAX_VAL;
107          fprintf(stderr, "  Http done  ");
108        }else{
109          total_count++;
110        }
111      }else{
112        rt.bytes_sent = hx_ev.file_size;
113        rt.status = ST_STAT(hx_ev.http.status);
114        memcpy((char *)rt.url, (const char *)hx_ev.http.url, 8);
115
116        /* Read the next helix event*/
117        if(fread(&hx_ev, sizeof(struct helix_event), 1, hx_file) != 1){
118          /* Reset the impoortant structures if EOF reached*/
119          fclose(hx_file);
120          hx_file = NULL;
121          hx_ev.http.abstime = TIME_MAX_VAL;
122          fprintf(stderr, "  Helix done  ");
123        }else{
124          total_count++;
125        }
126      }
127
128      /* Check if reached EOF on both inputs */
129      if((ht_file == NULL) && (hx_file == NULL))
130        break;
131
132      const char *urlstr = hash_url.get(*(url_key*)&rt.url);
133      if(!urlstr) {
134        printf("url hash not found. SHOULD NOT HAPPEN!\n");
135        return 2;
136      }
137
138      if(total_count % 10000 == 0){
139        fprintf(stderr, ".");
140      }
141
142      if((rt.status != 304) && (rt.status != 200)){
143        status_count++;
144        continue;
145      }
146
147      /* Zero-length 200 entries are preserved in case they are needed
148       * later.
149       */
150
151      if(!isValidURL(urlstr)){
152        invalid_count++;
153        continue;
154      }
155
156      if(fwrite(&rt, sizeof(struct raw_trace), 1, out_file) != 1){
157        printf("Error writing to trace!\n");
158        break;
159      }
160    } //for
161
162    printf("\r%llu total entries found.\n"
163           "%llu discarded due to wrong status value. \n"
164           " of the remaining entries %llu discarded "
165           "due to URL limitation.\n"
166           "%llu valid entries remain.\n",
167           total_count, status_count, invalid_count,
168           total_count - (status_count + invalid_count));
169
170
171    fprintf(stderr, "\n");
172    fclose(out_file);
173
174    return 0;
175  }
```

C.3.3   mkalloctrc.h

```
1  #ifndef MKALLOCTRC_H
2  #define MKALLOCTRC_H
```

```
 3
 4
 5   /*
 6    * Structures used to represent file events and skip list entries.
 7    * Skip list is used to store files, ordered by its URL hash value.
 8    * Only "insert" operation is implemented as we never search for or
 9    * delete from the skip list. Each entry in the skip list can
10    * represent several files, as a file can be created, deleted and then
11    * a file with the same name, but of different size can be created in
12    * its place. For this purpose we keep a pointer to the last, active
13    * file in the file node. The remaining, inactive files are only
14    * accessible through the next pointers in the file entry structures.
15    * When allocation trace is finally committed to disk, we traverse the
16    * list using a specially maintained next pointer, which orders the
17    * files by their creation "tick" time.
18    */
19
20   /* Skip list maximum height, based on the expected number of nodes in
21    * the list and the used level probability factor:
22    *    2^MAXLEVEL approx.= number_of_nodes
23    * levels range from (0 .. MAXLEVEL)
24    */
25
26
27   /*
28    * Structure describing a file, by its name and containing a pointer
29    * to the last instance of that file.
30    */
31   struct file_node{
32     struct file_ent  *file;          //The last active file
33     unsigned long       replacements; //Number of file replacements within
34                                        //a node.
35     unsigned char     url[8];         //Sorting key
36   } __attribute__((packed));
37
38
39   /*
40    * File entry properties that describe a file. In_tick is only used to
41    * calculate a file's out_tick in certain cases — it is never stored.
42    */
43   struct file_ent{
44     unsigned int     size;
45     unsigned long    in_tick;
46     unsigned long    out_tick;
47     unsigned char    states;
48   };
49
50   /* Function prototypes */
51   struct file_ent *new_entry(struct raw_trace *trc,
52                              struct file_ent *prev_file);
53   int insert(struct raw_trace *trc);
54   void build_data(char *filename);
55   void repl_dist(char *filename);
56   void alloc_trc(char *filename);
57
58   #endif
```

C.3.4   mkalloctrc.c

```
 1   #include <stdlib.h>
 2   #include <stdio.h>
 3   #include <string.h>
 4   #include <time.h>
 5
 6   #include "../common/storage_types.h"
 7   #include "skiplist.h"
 8
 9   #include "mkalloctrc.h"
10
11   /*
12    * Global values
13    */
14
15   //Two skip lists are maintaind:
16   struct skip_list g_file_list;
17   //, which is ordered by URL and contains the information about the
18   //currently active files and
19
20   struct skip_list g_ent_list;
21   //, whic is a list of file entries. Every file entry is placed here,
```

```
22   //based on its insertion tick time.
23
24   //Each time a new file instance is observed, the ticks counter is
25   //advanced by one.
26   unsigned long g_ticks;
27
28   unsigned long g_replacements, g_discarded;
29   //high watermarks
30   unsigned long long g_allocated_max;
31
32
33   /*
34    * Compare functions for the skip lists:
35    */
36
37   /* File list: */
38   int filelist_comp(const void *val1, const void *val2){
39     return memcmp(((struct file_node *)val1)->url,
40                    ((struct file_node *)val2)->url,
41                    8);
42   }
43
44
45   /* Entry list: */
46   int entlist_comp(const void *val1, const void *val2){
47     if(((struct file_ent *)val1)->in_tick >
48        ((struct file_ent *)val2)->in_tick)
49       return 1;
50
51     if(((struct file_ent *)val1)->in_tick <
52        ((struct file_ent *)val2)->in_tick)
53       return -1;
54
55     return 0;
56
57   }
58
59   /* Entry list, compare by out_tick: */
60   int entlist_delcomp(const void *val1, const void *val2){
61     if(((struct file_ent *)val1)->out_tick >
62        ((struct file_ent *)val2)->out_tick)
63       return 1;
64
65     if(((struct file_ent *)val1)->out_tick <
66        ((struct file_ent *)val2)->out_tick)
67       return -1;
68
69     return 0;
70
71   }
72
73
74
75   /* Create a new file entry and initialise it with data from the raw
76    * trace. Global tick is incremented here!
77    */
78   struct file_ent *new_entry(struct raw_trace *trc,
79                              struct file_ent *prev_file){
80     struct file_ent *tmp_ent;
81     static unsigned long long allocated_running = 0;
82     statusEnum_t res;
83
84     if((tmp_ent = malloc(sizeof(struct file_ent))) == NULL){
85       fprintf(stderr, "Out_of_memory_in_new_entry\n");
86       exit(1);
87     }
88
89     g_ticks++;
90
91     tmp_ent->size = trc->bytes_sent;
92     tmp_ent->in_tick = g_ticks;
93     tmp_ent->out_tick = 0;
94     tmp_ent->states = 0;
95
96     res = sl_insert_node(&g_ent_list, tmp_ent);
97     if(res != SL_OK){
98       fprintf(stderr, "Error_inserting_new_node_in_new_entry().\n");
99       exit(res);
100    }
101
102    //In case of replacement, unconditionally set the deletion time of
103    //the previous instance of the file to the preceeding tick time.
104    if(prev_file != NULL){
```

162

```c
105        allocated_running -= prev_file->size;
106        prev_file->states |= FL_REPLACED;
107        prev_file->out_tick = g_ticks - 1;
108      }
109
110      //Compute high watermarks for the number of bytes allocated.
111      allocated_running += trc->bytes_sent;
112      if(allocated_running > g_allocated_max)
113        g_allocated_max = allocated_running;
114
115      return tmp_ent;
116   }
117
118
119   /***********************************************
120    *   allocate node for data and insert in list  *
121    ***********************************************/
122   int insert(struct raw_trace *trc){
123     struct file_node dummy;
124     struct file_node *x;
125     statusEnum_t res;
126
127     // Check if the file with the given URL is already present
128     memcpy(dummy.url, trc->url, 8);
129     x = sl_find_node(&g_file_list, &dummy, &res);
130
131     // If not, we insert a new file_node
132     if(res != SL_OK){
133       /* If resent of an uninitialised entry -- ignore */
134       if(trc->status == 304){
135         g_discarded++;
136         return 0;
137       }
138
139       /* make new node */
140       x = malloc(sizeof(struct file_node));
141       if (x == NULL){
142         fprintf(stderr, "Out_of_memory_in_insert.\n");
143         exit(1);
144       }
145
146       memcpy(x->url, trc->url, 8);
147       x->file = new_entry(trc, NULL);
148       x->replacements = 0;
149
150       res = sl_insert_node(&g_file_list, x);
151       if(res != SL_OK){
152         fprintf(stderr, "Error_inserting_new_node_in_insert().\n");
153         exit(res);
154       }
155
156     }else{
157       // The URL node already exists -- check the active file.
158       switch(trc->status){
159       case 200:
160         //In case the file size changed, insert a new file entry at the
161         //same node: the old entry becomes only reachable through
162         //ent_list skiplist.
163         if(x->file->size != trc->bytes_sent){
164           g_replacements++;
165           x->replacements++;
166           x->file = new_entry(trc, x->file);
167           return 0;
168         }
169         /* else FALLTHROUGH and update */
170       case 304:
171         x->file->out_tick = g_ticks;
172         return 0; //nothing to insert
173       default:
174         fprintf(stderr,
175                 "Switch_in_insert:_unreachable_reached_(status_=_%d).\n"
176                 "Raw_trace_is_corrupt!\n", trc->status);
177         exit(1);
178       }; //switch
179     }
180
181     return 0;
182   }
183
184
185   /*
186    * Go through the binary filtered weblog and generate file entries.
187    */
```

163

```
188   void build_data(char *filename){
189     FILE *fin;
190     unsigned long discarded_zero;
191     unsigned long long total_count = 0;
192     struct raw_trace rt;
193
194     fprintf(stderr, "Reading raw_trace and building datastructures ");
195
196     if((fin = fopen(filename, "r")) == NULL){
197       fprintf(stderr, "Cannot open binary firltered trace!\n");
198       exit(1);
199     }
200
201     discarded_zero = 0;
202     for(;;){
203       if(fread(&rt, sizeof(struct raw_trace), 1, fin) != 1){
204         fprintf(stderr, "done.\n\n");
205         break;
206       }
207
208       total_count++;
209       if(total_count % 10000 == 0)
210         fprintf(stderr, ".");
211
212       if((rt.bytes_sent == 0) && (rt.status == 200))
213         discarded_zero++;
214       else
215         insert(&rt);
216
217     } //for
218
219     fclose(fin);
220
221     printf("Total entries in raw trace:\t\t%llu\n", total_count);
222     printf("Creation operations:\t\t\t%lu\n", g_ticks);
223     printf("Replacements found:\t\t\t%lu\n", g_replacements);
224     printf("Discarded not_alloc'ed 304 entries:\t%lu\n", g_discarded);
225     printf("Discarded 0-length, size 200 entries:\t%lu\n", discarded_zero);
226     printf("Skiplist: filenode listlevel:\t\t%d\n",
227            g_file_list.maxListLevel);
228     printf("Skiplist: unique file URLs:\t\t%lu\n",
229            g_ticks - g_replacements);
230     printf("Estimated maximum allocated bytes:\t%llu\n", g_allocated_max);
231
232   }
233
234
235   /*
236    * Linearly go though the filename list and print replacement
237    * distribution.
238    */
239   void repl_dist(char *filename){
240     FILE *fout;
241     char *name_tmp;
242     unsigned long i, del_adjusted = 0;
243     struct list_node *ln_tmp;
244     struct file_node *fn_tmp;
245
246     fprintf(stderr, "Writing replacement distribution file ... ");
247     name_tmp = malloc(strlen(filename + 7));
248     sprintf(name_tmp, "%s.rdist", filename);
249
250     if((fout = fopen(name_tmp, "w")) == NULL){
251       fprintf(stderr, "Cannot open output rdist file!\n");
252       exit(1);
253     }
254     free(name_tmp);
255
256     i = 0;
257
258     /* We dump all file nodes to a binary file (the value in the file
259      * member obviously becomes meaningless). Another application is used
260      * to generate an ASCII file containing the number of replacements
261      * along with the corresponding URL names.
262      */
263     ln_tmp = g_file_list.hdr->forward[0];
264     while(ln_tmp != g_file_list.nil){
265       fn_tmp = (struct file_node *)(ln_tmp->data);
266       fwrite(fn_tmp, sizeof(struct file_node), 1, fout);
267
268       /* In the process we also adjust the deletion times if it is the
269        * last file in the log.
270        */
```

```
271      if(fn_tmp->file->out_tick == 0){
272        del_adjusted++;
273        fn_tmp->file->states != FL_DELMOD;
274        fn_tmp->file->out_tick =
275          fn_tmp->file->in_tick + ((g_ticks - fn_tmp->file->in_tick)/3)*2;
276      }
277
278      ln_tmp = ln_tmp->forward[0];
279    };
280
281    fclose(fout);
282    fprintf(stderr, "_done.\n");
283
284    printf("\nAdjusted_0-length_lifetimes:\t\t%lu\n", del_adjusted);
285  }
286
287
288  /*
289   * Generate the allocation trace itself
290   */
291  void alloc_trc(char *filename){
292    FILE *fout;
293    struct file_ent *fe_in, *fe_out;
294    struct list_node *ln_in, *ln_out;
295    struct alloc_trace at;
296    unsigned long del_rest = 0;
297
298    struct skip_list del_list;
299    statusEnum_t res;
300
301    fprintf(stderr, "Sorting_deletion_times..._");
302
303    /* We first re-sort file entries by the deletion tick. Several
304       deletions can fall on the same tick. After the resorting, the
305       same nodes are present in both lists. */
306    if(sl_initList(&del_list, 32, TRUE, &entlist_delcomp) != SL_OK){
307      fprintf(stderr, "Error_while_initialising_deletion_list!\n");
308      exit(1);;
309    }
310
311    ln_in = g_ent_list.hdr->forward[0];
312    while(ln_in != g_ent_list.nil){
313      res = sl_insert_node(&del_list, ln_in->data);
314      if(res != SL_OK){
315        fprintf(stderr,
316                "Error_while_inserting_entry_into_deletion_list.\n");
317        exit(res);
318      }
319
320      ln_in = ln_in->forward[0];
321    }; //while
322
323    fprintf(stderr, "done.\n");
324
325    printf("Skiplist:_entlist_listlevel:\t\t%d\n", g_ent_list.maxListLevel);
326    printf("Skiplist:_dellist_listlevel:\t\t%d\n", del_list.maxListLevel);
327
328    fprintf(stderr, "Writing_allocation_trace_");
329
330
331    if((fout = fopen(filename, "w")) == NULL){
332      fprintf(stderr, "Cannot_open_output_file!\n");
333      exit(1);
334    }
335
336    /* We now go through all registered ticks again, writing to the
337     * trace first an allocation command, followed by zero or more
338     * deallocation commands.
339     */
340    ln_in = g_ent_list.hdr->forward[0];
341    ln_out = del_list.hdr->forward[0];
342    while(ln_in != g_ent_list.nil){
343      //Bit 1 is set if the file entry was replaced by another size.
344      //Bit 5 is set if deleted value is adjusted
345      fe_in = (struct file_ent *)(ln_in->data);
346      at.flags = fe_in->states | OP_CREATE;
347      at.size = fe_in->size;
348      at.file_id = fe_in->in_tick;
349      fwrite(&at, sizeof(struct alloc_trace), 1, fout);
350
351      //Now locate and write all deletion events for this tick
352      at.flags = OP_DELETE;
353      at.size = 0;
```

165

```
354    while((ln_out != del_list.nil) &&
355          (((struct file_ent *)(ln_out->data))->out_tick ==
356          fe_in->in_tick)){
357
358      fe_out = (struct file_ent *)(ln_out->data);
359
360      //Count remaining zero-length lifetimes
361      if(fe_out->in_tick == fe_out->out_tick)
362        del_rest++;
363
364      at.file_id = fe_out->in_tick;
365      fwrite(&at, sizeof(struct alloc_trace), 1, fout);
366
367      ln_out = ln_out->forward[0];
368    }; //while(ln_out...
369
370    if(fe_in->in_tick % 10000 == 0)
371      fprintf(stderr, ".");
372
373    ln_in = ln_in->forward[0];
374  }; //while(ln_in...
375
376  fclose(fout);
377  fprintf(stderr, "_done.\n\n");
378  printf("Remaining_0-length_lifetimes:\t\t%lu\n", del_rest);
379 }
380
381
382 int main(int argc, char **argv){
383   g_discarded = g_replacements = 0;
384   g_ticks = 0;
385   g_allocated_max = 0;
386
387   if(argc != 3){
388     fprintf(stderr,
389             "Argument_mismatch\nUsage:_%s_in_trace_out_trace\n",
390             strrchr(argv[0], '/')+1);
391     exit(1);
392   }
393
394   /************************************************/
395
396
397   if((sl_initList(&g_file_list, 20, FALSE, &filelist_comp) != SL_OK) ||
398      (sl_initList(&g_ent_list, 32, FALSE, &entlist_comp) != SL_OK)){
399     fprintf(stderr, "Error_while_initialising_lists!\n");
400     return 1;
401   }
402
403
404   /************************************************/
405
406   build_data(argv[1]);
407
408   /** Print replacement and adjust del times ********/
409
410   repl_dist(argv[2]);
411
412   /************************************************/
413
414   alloc_trc(argv[2]);
415
416   return 0;
417 }
```

C.3.5 print_repl.cc

```
 1 #ifdef WITH_URLS
 2 #include "../scripts/client_event.h"
 3 #include "../scripts/stt/stage_bdb_map.h"
 4 #endif
 5
 6 #include <stdio.h>
 7 #include <stdlib.h>
 8 #include <string.h>
 9
10 #include "mkalloctrc.h"
11 #include "../common/libarg.h"
12
13 int main(int argc, char **argv){
```

```
14    struct file_node fnode;
15    FILE *in_file = NULL;
16    char *param;
17    unsigned long limit = 0;
18
19    /* Parse the arguements */
20    if(parseArgs(argc, argv, "-f", FALSE, &param) && (param != NULL)){
21        if((in_file = fopen(param, "r")) == NULL){
22            fprintf(stderr, "Cannot_open_binary_replacement_log!\n");
23            return 1;
24        }
25    }
26
27    /* Lower boundary for the number of replacements */
28    if(parseArgs(argc, argv, "-l", FALSE, &param) && (param != NULL)){
29        limit = atol(param);
30    }
31
32 #ifdef WITH_URLS
33    /* Must be the last arg check as param value is used later */
34    parseArgs(argc, argv, "-d", FALSE, &param);
35
36    if((param == NULL) || (in_file == NULL)){
37        fprintf(stderr, "Usage:\r0%s_-f_replacement_log_-l_lower_limit_"
38            "-d_hash_db\n", argv[0]);
39        return 1;
40    }
41
42    /* Open the URL database */
43    bdb db(param, DB_UNKNOWN, DB_RDONLY);
44    bdb_map<url_key, char*> hash_url(db);
45 #else
46    if(in_file == NULL){
47        fprintf(stderr, "Usage:\r0%s_-f_replacement_log_-l_lower_limit\n",
48            argv[0]);
49        return 1;
50    }
51 #endif
52
53    //Read the log and output the text version on stdout
54    for(;;){
55        if(fread(&fnode, sizeof(struct file_node), 1, in_file) != 1){
56            fprintf(stderr, "Reading_done.\n\n");
57            break;
58        }
59
60        if(fnode.replacements < limit)
61            continue;
62
63 #ifdef WITH_URLS
64        const char *urlstr = hash_url.get(*(url_key*)&fnode.url);
65        if(!urlstr) {
66            fprintf(stderr, "url_hash_not_found._SHOULD_NOT_HAPPEN!\n");
67            return 2;
68        }
69
70        printf("%lu\t%s\n", fnode.replacements, urlstr);
71 #else
72        printf("%lu\n", fnode.replacements);
73 #endif
74    } //for(;;)
75
76    return 0;
77 }
```

C.3.6 Makefile

```
1  PROGS=mkalloctrc clean_trace print_repl print_repl_nourl
2  CC_OPTS=-Wall -g
3
4  .PHONY: all clean realclean remake
5
6  all: $(PROGS)
7
8  remake: realclean all
9
10 clean:
11         rm -f *.o *~
12         rm -f core *.stackdump
```

167

```
13
14  realclean: clean
15          rm -f $(PROGS)
16
17
18  clean_trace: clean_trace.cc ../common/storage_types.h libarg.o
19          g++ -Wall -O2 -I/usr/pkg/include -L/usr/pkg/lib -o $@\
20              clean_trace.cc ../scripts/stt/stage_bdb.o libarg.o -ldb4_cxx
21
22  print_repl: print_repl.cc mkalloctrc.h libarg.o
23          g++ -Wall -O2 -DWITH_URLS -I/usr/pkg/include -L/usr/pkg/lib -o $@\
24              print_repl.cc ../scripts/stt/stage_bdb.o libarg.o -ldb4_cxx
25
26  print_repl_nourl: print_repl.cc mkalloctrc.h libarg.o
27          g++ -Wall -O2 -o $@ print_repl.cc libarg.o
28
29  mkalloctrc: mkalloctrc.c ../common/storage_types.h skiplist.h \
30              mkalloctrc.h skiplist.o
31          gcc -O3 $(CC_OPTS) -o $@  mkalloctrc.c skiplist.o
32
33  skiplist.o: skiplist.c skiplist.h
34          gcc $(CC_OPTS) -c $<
35
36  libarg.o: ../common/libarg.c ../common/libarg.h
37          g++ $(CC_OPTS) -c $<
```

C.4 File Size Distribution Analyser

This is the source code of our suite used to evaluate file size distribution. `fsize_sys.c` and `fsize_trc.c` contain functions to collect information either from an existing file system or from a trace. They make use of functions found in `fsize_scan.c` to parse and present the raw information. `fsize_stat.c` holds the functions that read the output produced by either `fsize_sys.c` or `fsize_trc.c` and gathers statistical information about the file size distribution. If instructed, it can also group file sizes into bins, thus simulating the segregation behaviour of QuickFit allocation algorithm and allowing us to forecast the expected load on the quick lists.

C.4.1 fsize_scan.h

```
1  #ifndef FSIZE_SCAN_H
2  #define FSIZE_SCAN_H
3
4  unsigned long glob_count;
5
6  struct statentry{
7    unsigned long grain_size;
8    unsigned long count;
9    struct statentry *forward[1]; /* skip list forward pointer */
10 };
11
12 //Skip list datastructures
13 #define MAXLEVEL 25
14
15 struct SkipList {
16    struct statentry *hdr;            /* list Header */
17    int listLevel;                    /* current level of list */
18 } SkipList;
19
20 //SkipList g_list;                   /* skip list information */
21
22 #define NIL list->hdr
23
24 //Function prototypes
25 void errstop(char *msg, int code);
26 void insert_count(struct SkipList *list, unsigned long grain);
27 void printstat(struct SkipList *list);
28 void initList(struct SkipList *list);
29
30 #endif
```

C.4.2 fsize_scan.c

```
1  #include <stdlib.h>
2  #include <stdio.h>
3  #include <time.h>
4
5  #include "fsize_scan.h"
6
7  void errstop(char *msg, int code){
8    fprintf(stderr, "fsize_scan_stopped_with_code_%id:\n\t%s\n", code, msg);
9    exit(code);
10 }
11
12 void printstat(struct SkipList *list){
13   struct statentry *tmp;
```

```
14
15    //Print statistics to stdout and free entries
16    tmp = list->hdr->forward[0];
17    do{
18      if(tmp->count != 0){ //Exclude head entry if empty
19        fprintf(stdout, "%lu\t%lu\n", tmp->grain_size, tmp->count);
20      }
21
22      tmp = tmp->forward[0];
23    }while(tmp != NIL);
24
25    fprintf(stderr, "\nTotal_files_scanned:_%lu\n", glob_count);
26 }
27
28
29 /** Skip List Functions **/
30
31
32 /* Determine random level for the new skip list node. "Fix the dice"
33  * by allowing the new level to be at most one more than the current
34  * level of the list.
35  */
36 static int get_level(struct SkipList *list){
37    int newLevel;
38
39    for(
40        newLevel = 0;
41        rand() < RAND_MAX/2
42          && newLevel < MAXLEVEL
43          && newLevel <= list->listLevel + 1;
44        newLevel++);
45
46    return newLevel;
47 }
48
49
50
51 void insert_count(struct SkipList *list, unsigned long grain){
52    int i, newLevel;
53    struct statentry *update[MAXLEVEL+1];
54    struct statentry *x;
55
56    /**************************************************
57     * allocate node for data and insert in list *
58     **************************************************/
59
60    /* find where key belongs */
61    x = list->hdr;
62    for (i = list->listLevel; i >= 0; i--) {
63      while (x->forward[i] != NIL
64          && x->forward[i]->grain_size < grain)
65        x = x->forward[i];
66      update[i] = x;
67    }
68
69    //If the entry already exists, update its count.
70    x = x->forward[0];
71    if (x != NIL && x->grain_size == grain) {
72      x->count++;
73      return;
74    }
75
76    /* determine level */
77    newLevel = get_level(list);
78    if (newLevel > list->listLevel) {
79      for (i = list->listLevel + 1; i <= newLevel; i++)
80        update[i] = NIL;
81      list->listLevel = newLevel;
82    }
83
84    /* make new node */
85    x = malloc(sizeof(struct statentry) + newLevel *
86              sizeof(struct statentry *));
87
88    if (x == NULL){
89      printf("Out_of_memory_in_insert.\n");
90      exit(1);
91    }
92
93    x->grain_size = grain;
94    x->count = 1;
95
96    /* update forward links */
```

```
97      for (i = 0; i <= newLevel; i++) {
98        x->forward[i] = update[i]->forward[i];
99        update[i]->forward[i] = x;
100     }
101  }
102
103
104  void initList(struct SkipList *list){
105    int i;
106
107    list->hdr = malloc(sizeof(struct statentry) + MAXLEVEL *
108                       sizeof(struct statentry *));
109    if (list->hdr == NULL) {
110      printf ("insufficient_memory_(initList)\n");
111      exit(1);
112    }
113    for (i = 0; i <= MAXLEVEL; i++)
114      list->hdr->forward[i] = NIL;
115    list->listLevel = 0;
116
117    srand(time(NULL));
118  }
```

C.4.3   fsize_sys.c

```
1   /*
2    * Collect the file count information for each of the sizes present in
3    * a system, starting from a specified location.
4    */
5
6   #include <stdlib.h>
7
8   #include <sys/stat.h>
9   #include <fcntl.h>
10
11  #include <sys/types.h>
12  #include <dirent.h>
13
14  #include <unistd.h>
15
16  #include <stdio.h>
17  #include <string.h>
18
19  #include "fsize_scan.h"
20
21  void statdir(char *dir, struct SkipList *list){
22    DIR *fdir;
23    struct dirent *dentry;
24    struct stat buf;
25    char *fname;
26    static int depth = 0;
27
28    //Attempt opening the given directory
29    if((fdir = opendir(dir)) == NULL)
30      return;
31    else
32      depth++;
33
34    //Set cut-off for progress reporting
35    if(depth < 4)
36      fprintf(stderr, "Reading %s\n", dir);
37
38    //The big loop to read all directory entries
39    while((dentry = readdir(fdir)) != NULL){
40      //Prepend the file name with a full path
41      fname = malloc(strlen(dir) + strlen(dentry->d_name) + 2);
42      sprintf(fname, "%s/%s", dir, dentry->d_name);
43
44      //Get file info without following symbolic links,
45      //thus reading info only once per file.
46      lstat(fname, &buf);
47
48      //Recursevly read subdirectories.
49      //Exclude 'procfs', '.' and '..'
50      if(S_ISDIR(buf.st_mode) && (strstr(fname, "/proc/") == NULL) &&
51         !(dentry->d_name[0] == '.' &&
52          (dentry->d_name[1] == '.' || dentry->d_name[1] == '\0')
53          )){
54        statdir(fname, list);
55      }
```

171

```
56      //Only read the size of regular files
57      if(S_ISREG(buf.st_mode)){
58        insert_count(list , (unsigned long)buf.st_size);
59        glob_count++;
60      }
61
62
63      free(fname);
64    }//while
65
66    closedir(fdir);
67    depth--;
68  }
69
70
71  int main(int argc, char **argv){
72    struct SkipList list;
73
74    if(argc < 2)
75      errstop("Insufficient_number_of_atrguments._Usage:_\n"
76              "\tfsize_scan_root_dir", 1);
77
78    initList(&list);
79
80    //Collect statistics
81    statdir(argv[1], &list);
82    printstat(&list);
83
84    return 0;
85  }
```

C.4.4   fsize_trc.c

```
1  /*
2   * Collect the file count information for each of the sizes present in
3   * a given allocation trace.
4   */
5
6  #include <stdlib.h>
7
8  #include <sys/stat.h>
9  #include <fcntl.h>
10
11  #include <sys/types.h>
12  #include <dirent.h>
13
14  #include <unistd.h>
15
16  #include <stdio.h>
17  #include <string.h>
18
19  #include "fsize_scan.h"
20
21  #include "../common/libarg.h" //For argument parsing
22  #include "../common/storage_types.h"
23
24  int g_with_replacements;
25
26  void stattrc(FILE *fin, struct SkipList *list){
27    struct alloc_trace at;
28
29    fprintf(stderr, "Reading_trace_file.\n");
30    for(;;){
31      if(fread(&at, sizeof(struct alloc_trace), 1, fin) != 1){
32        fprintf(stderr, "Reading_done.\n\n");
33        break;
34      }
35
36      //Ignore "detele" operation entries
37      if(at.flags & OP_DELETE)
38        continue;
39
40      if(g_with_replacements){
41        insert_count(list , at.size);
42        glob_count++;
43      }else{
44        //Depending on the option, ignore entries with "replaced" bit set
45        if(!(at.flags & FL_REPLACED)){
46          insert_count(list , at.size);
47          glob_count++;
```

172

```
48          }
49       }
50    } //for
51  }
52
53
54  int main(int argc, char **argv){
55     struct SkipList list;
56     char *param;
57     FILE *fin = NULL;
58
59     g_with_replacements = parseArgs(argc, argv, "-r", TRUE, NULL);
60
61     //Read the file name containing data.
62     if(parseArgs(argc, argv, "-f", FALSE, &param) && (param != NULL)){
63       if((fin = fopen(param, "r")) == NULL){
64         errstop("Cannot_open_input_trace!\n", 2);
65       }
66     }
67
68     if(fin == NULL)
69       errstop("Insufficient_number_of_atrguments.\n"
70               "Usage:\tfsize_trc_-f_tracefile_[-r]\n"
71               "-r_switch_denotes_if_the_replaced_files_"
72               "should_be_counted_in.\n",
73               1);
74
75
76     initList(&list);
77
78     //Collect statistics
79     stattrc(fin, &list);
80     printstat(&list);
81
82     return 0;
83  }
```

C.4.5 fsize_stat.c

```
1  /*
2   * Parse the information collected by fsize_scan and present
3   * statistical information about file size distribution, based on
4   * storage allocation granularity size., suitable for plotting. Also
5   * presents the totals information.
6   */
7
8  #include <limits.h>
9  #include <stdio.h>
10 #include <stdlib.h>
11 #include <string.h>
12
13 #include "../common/libarg.h" //For argument parsing
14
15 #define MBYTES(x) ((x)/1048576.0)
16 #define GBYTES(x) ((x)/1073741824.0)
17
18 struct statentry{
19    unsigned long grain_size;
20    unsigned long count;
21    struct statentry *next;
22 };
23
24 void errstop(char *msg, int code){
25    fprintf(stderr, "fsize_stat_stopped_with_code_%d:\n\t%s\n", code, msg);
26    exit(code);
27 }
28
29
30 /* Adjust the size of the request up to the nearest multiple of the
31  * grain size, taking into account the space required for the extent
32  * header.
33  */
34 inline unsigned long long adjust_size(unsigned long long fsize,
35                                       unsigned long header_size,
36                                       unsigned long grain_size){
37 //return ((fsize + header_size) / grain_size) * grain_size + grain_size;
38    return fsize + header_size;
39 }
40
41
```

173

```
42  void collect_stat(FILE *fin, unsigned long grain_size,
43                    unsigned long mlist_s, unsigned long header_size){
44    unsigned long long fsize = 0, fcount = 0;
45    unsigned long long cur_grain, glob_count, acc, mean, qlist_count, mlist_acc;
46    unsigned long long sum, sumgr;
47    int res = 0;
48    struct statentry *head, *cur, *prev, *max;
49
50    fprintf(stdout,"#Grains\tCount\t\t\tstart\t-_\tstop\n");
51
52    //Read stdin (or a given file) and condense statistics for specified
53    //grain size. We jump over the first line containig 0-length files
54    //as they do not count in the statistics for no space is allocated
55    //for such files.
56    if(fscanf(fin, "%llu\t%llu\n", &fsize, &fcount) == EOF){
57      errstop("Not_enough_input_data!", 2);
58    }
59
60    if(fsize == 0){
61      if(fscanf(fin, "%llu\t%llu\n", &fsize, &fcount) == EOF){
62        errstop("Not_enough_input_data!", 2);
63      }
64    }
65
66    fsize = adjust_size(fsize, header_size, grain_size);
67
68    cur = prev = head = max = malloc(sizeof(struct statentry));
69
70    acc = glob_count = mean = qlist_count = mlist_acc = 0;
71    sumgr = sum = 0;
72
73    cur_grain = 1;
74
75    for(;;){
76      //Switch to the next grain if the newly-read file size overflows
77      //the old one or the last entry is read from fin; print the
78      //accumulated statistics for the old grain.
79      if((acc && (fsize > cur_grain * grain_size)) || (res == EOF)){
80        fprintf(stdout, "%lu\t%llu\t\t%lu\t-_%lu\n",
81                cur_grain, acc,
82                cur_grain * grain_size - grain_size + 1,
83                cur_grain * grain_size);
84
85        //Compute bytes allocated for files using the given grain size.
86        sumgr += (unsigned long long)acc * cur_grain * grain_size;
87
88        cur->grain_size = cur_grain;
89        cur->count = acc;
90        cur->next = NULL;
91
92        //Compute the grain with the largest number of files in it
93        if(max->count < acc){
94          max = cur;
95        }
96
97        //Add a new quick list or increase the number of files in the
98        //misc list, depending on the files' size.
99        if(cur_grain * grain_size < mlist_s){
100         qlist_count++;
101       }else{
102         mlist_acc += acc;
103       }
104
105       //break the for(;;) loop in case of last entry
106       if(res == EOF) break;
107
108       cur = malloc(sizeof(struct statentry));
109       prev->next = cur;
110       prev = cur;
111
112       acc = 0;
113
114       //Calculate next grain size
115       cur_grain = fsize / grain_size;
116
117     } //end commit and advance
118
119     //Update counters and read next line only if the previously read
120     //values fit into the current grain, otherwise scan until a
121     //fitting grain is found.
122     if((fsize > cur_grain * grain_size - grain_size) &&
123        (fsize <= cur_grain * grain_size)){
124       acc += fcount;          //Accumulator for the current grain
```

174

```
125        glob_count += fcount;    //Total number of files
126        sum += fcount * fsize;   //Total number of bytes
127
128        res = fscanf(fin, "%llu\t%llu\n", &fsize, &fcount);
129        fsize = adjust_size(fsize, header_size, grain_size);
130      }else{
131        cur_grain++;
132      }
133    } //for(;;) loop broken after last time through is processed
134
135    //Calculate mean grain size
136    cur = head;
137    mean = 0;
138    do{
139      mean += cur->count;
140      if(mean >= glob_count / 2){
141        mean = cur->grain_size;
142        break;
143      }
144      cur = cur->next;
145    }while(cur != NULL);
146
147    fprintf(stdout, "\n");
148    fprintf(stdout,
149        "#_Total_of_%lluB_/_%0.3fMB_/_%0.3fGB_in_%llu_files_scanned.\n",
150        sum, MBYTES(sum), GBYTES(sum), glob_count);
151    fprintf(stdout,
152        "#_Average_file_size:\t\t%0.2Lf_bytes\n",
153        sum / (long double)glob_count);
154    fprintf(stdout, "#_1_Grain_=\t\t\t%llu_bytes\n", grain_size);
155    fprintf(stdout, "#_Header_size_=\t\t\t%llu_bytes\n", header_size);
156
157    if(grain_size == 1){ // Byte-level menings are slightly different
158      fprintf(stdout,
159          "#_Number_of_unique_file_sizes:\t%llu_,_"
160          "with_%llu_files_above_%llu_bytes.\n",
161          qlist_count + mlist_acc, mlist_acc, mlist_s);
162      fprintf(stdout, "#_50%%_of_files_are_<=\t\t%llu_bytes\n", mean);
163      fprintf(stdout, "#_Most_files_are\t\t%llu_bytes_long_(%llu_files)\n",
164          max->grain_size, max->count);
165    }else{
166      fprintf(stdout, "#_Number_of_Quick_Lists:\t%llu\n", qlist_count);
167      fprintf(stdout,
168          "#_Misc_List_contains\t\t%llu_blocks_"
169          "above_%llu_bytes_in_size.\n",
170          mlist_acc, mlist_s);
171      fprintf(stdout, "#_50%%_of_files_occupy_<=\t%llu_grains\n", mean);
172      fprintf(stdout, "#_Highest_file_count_uses:\t"
173          "%llu_grains_in_interval_%llu_bytes_(%llu_files)\n",
174          max->grain_size,
175          max->grain_size * grain_size - grain_size + 1,
176          max->grain_size * grain_size,
177          max->count);
178    }
179    //Bytes allocated (sumgr) / bytes requested (sum)
180    fprintf(stdout,
181        "#_Internal_frag._ratio:\t\t\t"
182        "%0.6Lf_(%llu_alloc_/_%llu_req.)\n",
183        (long double)sumgr / sum, sumgr, sum);
184    fprintf(stdout,
185        "#_Lost_due_to_int._frag.:\t"
186        "%lluB_/_%0.3fMB_/_%0.3fGB_(%0.4Lf%%)\n",
187        sumgr - sum, MBYTES(sumgr - sum), GBYTES(sumgr - sum),
188        (sumgr - sum) * 100 / (long double)sumgr);
189    fprintf(stdout, "\n");
190
191 }
192
193
194 int main(int argc, char **argv){
195    FILE *fin;
196    int grain = 0;
197    unsigned long mlist = 0;
198    unsigned long header_size = 0;
199    char *param;
200
201    //Read the file name containing raw data. If the name is absent or
202    //is given as '=' then read stdin.
203    if(parseArgs(argc, argv, "-f", FALSE, &param) && (param != NULL)){
204      if(strcmp(param, "=") == 0){
205        fin = stdin;
206      }else if((fin = fopen(param, "r")) == NULL){
207        errstop("File_not_found\n", 3);
```

```
208      }
209    }else{
210      fin = stdin;
211    }
212
213    //Read the grain size value. This value must be present.
214    if(parseArgs(argc, argv, "-g", FALSE, &param) && (param != NULL)){
215      grain = atol(param);
216      if(grain <= 0){
217        errstop("Invalid_grain_size._Must_be_>_0.\n", 4);
218      }
219    }else{
220      errstop("Insufficient_number_of_atrguments._Usage:_\n"
221              "\tfsize_stat_-g_grain_size_[-f_in_file]_-]_"
222              "[-h_header_size]_[-m_misclist_size]\n"
223              "If_no_in_file_given,_stdin_is_read.\n", 1);
224    }
225
226
227    //Read the cut-off size for "misc list". The blocks larger than this
228    //size are placed in "misc list" thus reducin the number of exact
229    //quick lists in use. If the value is not given, the program assumes
230    //the largest possible unsigned long value. If a file size exceeds
231    //this value it will always be placed in a "misc list".
232    if(parseArgs(argc, argv, "-m", FALSE, &param) && (param != NULL)){
233      mlist = atol(param);
234    }else{
235      mlist = ULONG_MAX;
236    }
237
238    //"Misc list" size is corrected (rounded down) to be a multiple of
239    //grain size.
240    mlist = (mlist / grain) * grain;
241
242
243    //Read the size of the header field that will be ontained within
244    //the extent. If absent, no header (size 0) is assumed.
245    if(parseArgs(argc, argv, "-h", FALSE, &param) && (param != NULL)){
246      header_size = atol(param);
247    }
248
249    if(header_size + 1 > grain){
250      errstop("Grain_size_must_be_one_larger_than_the_header_size\n"
251              "\tto_allow_for_at_least_one_byte_of_payload.\n", 5);
252    }
253
254    collect_stat(fin, grain, mlist, header_size);
255
256    return 0;
257  }
```

C.4.6 Makefile

```
 1  OPTS=-O3 -Wall
 2  LIBS=libarg.o
 3  PROGS=fsize_sys fsize_trc fsize_stat
 4
 5  .PHONY: all clean realclean
 6
 7  all: $(PROGS)
 8
 9  clean:
10          rm -f *.o *~
11          rm -f core *.stackdump
12
13  realclean: clean
14          rm -f $(PROGS)
15
16
17  fsize_sys: fsize_sys.o fsize_scan.o
18          gcc $(OPTS) -o $@ fsize_scan.o fsize_sys.o
19
20  fsize_trc: fsize_trc.o fsize_scan.o $(LIBS)
21          gcc $(OPTS) -o $@ $(LIBS) fsize_scan.o fsize_trc.o
22
23  fsize_stat: fsize_stat.o $(LIBS)
24          gcc $(OPTS) -o $@ $(LIBS) fsize_stat.o
25
26
27  libarg.o: ../common/libarg.c ../common/libarg.h
```

176

```
28          gcc $(OPTS) −c $<
29
30  fsize_trc.o: fsize_trc.c fsize_scan.h ../common/storage_types.h \
31          ../common/libarg.h
32          gcc $(OPTS) −c $<
33
34  fsize_sys.o: fsize_sys.c fsize_scan.h
35          gcc $(OPTS) −c $<
36
37  fsize_scan.o: fsize_scan.c fsize_scan.h
38          gcc $(OPTS) −c $<
39
40  fsize_stat.o: fsize_stat.c ../common/libarg.h
41          gcc $(OPTS) −c $<
```

Appendix D

Program Outputs

D.1 Trace Generation

These are the summary outputs from trace generation programs.

D.1.1 Binary Server Log Parser

```
166260066 total entries found.
7412340 discarded due to wrong status value,
of the remaining entries 19970678  discarded due to URL limitation.
138877048 valid entries remain.
```

D.1.2 Allocation Trace Generator

```
Total entries in raw trace: 138877047
Creation operations: 14353600
Replacements found: 14285671
Discarded not alloc'ed 304 entries: 3580
Discarded 0-length fsize 200 entries: 80620
Skiplist: filenode listlevel: 16
Skiplist: unique file URLs: 67929
Estimated maximum allocated bytes: 13416369932

Adjusted 0-length lifetimes: 18720
```

179

```
Skiplist: entlist listlevel: 22
Skiplist: dellist listlevel: 22
Remaining 0-length lifetimes: 1777651
```

D.2   Simulation Runs

Below you will find the summary outputs of simulation runs for each of the partition classes, with AWP set to zero grains.

D.2.1   Minimum Partition Class

```
Trace request high watermark: 4950202308 bytes
Adjusted allocator high watermark: 9684049 grains
Internal fragmentation (avg. at peak load): 1.00162231

Number of files in the trace: 14353600
Total number of extents allocated: 14360054
Number of multi-extent allocations: 14
File fragmentation (avg. extents / file): 1.00044964
File fragmentation (max. extents / file): 1.00082787
File fragmentation (by multi-ext. file count): 0.00009754 perce

Total write requests: 28781595

Total coalescings: 15
Coalescings leading to single allocation: 2
Coalescigs with no mergings: 0
Avoided coalescings: 1

*** Memory usage ***

Total access count: 29362036
Total usage hight watermark: 1142884
Total usage throughput: 178156828

misclist list high watermark: 4100
misclist list throughput: 169896
quick lists high watermark: 471328
```

```
quick lists throughput: 173904268
misc lists high watermark: 52176
misc lists throughput: 1869876
extent headers high watermark: 650784
extent headers throughput: 858416
coalescing list high watermark: 129448
coalescing list throughput: 1354372
```

D.2.2 Medium Partition Class

```
Trace request high watermark: 4950202308 bytes
Adjusted allocator high watermark: 9683950 grains
Internal fragmentation (avg. at peak load): 1.00161207

Number of files in the trace: 14353600
Total number of extents allocated: 14353705
Number of multi-extent allocations: 15
File fragmentation (avg. extents / file): 1.00000732
File fragmentation (max. extents / file): 1.00001053
File fragmentation (by multi-ext. file count): 0.00010450 percent

Total write requests: 28768861

Total coalescings: 16
Coalescings leading to single allocation: 2
Coalescigs with no mergings: 0
Avoided coalescings: 1

*** Memory usage ***

Total access count: 29365564
Total usage hight watermark: 1158728
Total usage throughput: 173996120

misclist list high watermark: 4064
misclist list throughput: 174536
quick lists high watermark: 489248
quick lists throughput: 169691108
misc lists high watermark: 52696
misc lists throughput: 1870104
```

extent headers high watermark: 649184
extent headers throughput: 856384
coalescing list high watermark: 127648
coalescing list throughput: 1403988

D.2.3 Large Partition Class

Trace request high watermark: 4950202308 bytes
Adjusted allocator high watermark: 9683949 grains
Internal fragmentation (avg. at peak load): 1.00161197

Number of files in the trace: 14353600
Total number of extents allocated: 14353634
Number of multi-extent allocations: 6
File fragmentation (avg. extents / file): 1.00000237
File fragmentation (max. extents / file): 1.00000341
File fragmentation (by multi-ext. file count): 0.00004180 perce

Total write requests: 28768461

Total coalescings: 5
Coalescings leading to single allocation: 0
Coalescigs with no mergings: 0
Avoided coalescings: 1

*** Memory usage ***

Total access count: 29147995
Total usage hight watermark: 1212720
Total usage throughput: 174500444

misclist list high watermark: 4644
misclist list throughput: 146532
quick lists high watermark: 510588
quick lists throughput: 170957776
misc lists high watermark: 55792
misc lists throughput: 1768728
extent headers high watermark: 825056
extent headers throughput: 865824
coalescing list high watermark: 252344

coalescing list throughput: 761584

D.2.4 Huge Partition Class

Trace request high watermark: 4950202308 bytes
Adjusted allocator high watermark: 9683949 grains
Internal fragmentation (avg. at peak load): 1.00161197

Number of files in the trace: 14353600
Total number of extents allocated: 14353600
Number of multi-extent allocations: 0
File fragmentation (avg. extents / file): 1.00000000
File fragmentation (max. extents / file): 1.00000000
File fragmentation (by multi-ext. file count): 0.00000000 percent

Total write requests: 28762752

Total coalescings: 0
Coalescings leading to single allocation: 0
Coalescigs with no mergings: 0
Avoided coalescings: 0

*** Memory usage ***

Total access count: 28894109
Total usage hight watermark: 1620824
Total usage throughput: 172674084

misclist list high watermark: 4276
misclist list throughput: 137928
quick lists high watermark: 670380
quick lists throughput: 169951304
misc lists high watermark: 57348
misc lists throughput: 1696020
extent headers high watermark: 888832
extent headers throughput: 888832
coalescing list high watermark: 0
coalescing list throughput: 0

D.2.5 Minimum Partition Class with Coalescing Disabled

```
Trace request high watermark: 4950202308 bytes
Adjusted allocator high watermark: 9684280 grains
Internal fragmentation (avg. at peak load): 1.00164621

Number of files in the trace: 14353600
Total number of extents allocated: 14374881
Number of multi-extent allocations: 42
File fragmentation (avg. extents / file): 1.00148262
File fragmentation (max. extents / file): 1.00273955
File fragmentation (by multi-ext. file count): 0.00029261 perce

Total write requests: 28805418

Total coalescings: 0
Coalescings leading to single allocation: 0
Coalescigs with no mergings: 0
Avoided coalescings: 0

*** Memory usage ***

Total access count: 28938307
Total usage hight watermark: 1639544
Total usage throughput: 174847004

misclist list high watermark: 5612
misclist list throughput: 152484
quick lists high watermark: 684924
quick lists throughput: 172066584
misc lists high watermark: 58512
misc lists throughput: 1737440
extent headers high watermark: 890496
extent headers throughput: 890496
coalescing list high watermark: 0
coalescing list throughput: 0
```